God Prepared
A Fish

*How God Transformed an Atheist
Adrenaline Junkie into a Bible Smuggler*

DARVIS McCOY

*Stonehaven Press
Oroville, CA 95966
2018*

Stonehaven Press
70 Harry Lane
Oroville, California 95966

ISBN 978-0-9898999-5-6

You may contact the author at contact@godpreparedafish.com

Dedication

For my wife, Donna, who is my adventure partner, webmaster, editor, business manager, computer expert, encourager, and so much more; and for my honorary daughters, Megan K., Natalie K., and Kelly W.

Table of Contents

Publisher's Foreword

Darvis McCoy paints his own life story in these pages with the passion of a true adrenaline junkie. He felt a supernatural burden to get his memoir in print—not simply because it is an incredible true story, but because it bears witness to the modern-day miracle-working power of God. As I worked with him in the preparation of this volume, he would often get chills up his spine as he relived frightening moments at the airport x-ray scanners in hostile anti-Christian countries. He would recoil as he spoke of gunfire in the streets near his hotel. He would re-experience the poverty of "accommodations" without electricity, water, or even a toilet. When we would mention the names of the characters you will read about in this book, he would be overcome with love and compassion for the precious believers who face horrible persecution. He truly has spilled his heart on these pages. Darvis loves God. And Darvis deeply loves God's children in persecuted countries.

Yet as Darvis tells his story—which at times is gut-wrenching, the adrenaline junkie is able to keep his tongue planted in his cheek and make the reader smile. If you're like me, you'll find his wry humor cathartic amid the backdrop of such grim circumstances and happenings.

I have never known anyone quite like Darvis. See if you don't agree with me after you read this book.

Let me caution the reader regarding the nature of this volume. It tells of Darvis' forays into places where it isn't safe to be identified as a follower of Jesus. Many details of the story are intentionally missing for the safety of the persecuted believers. What you read here is absolutely true; it's simply not the whole story.

I am humbled to be a part of this monumental message to the church.

Ron Kingham
Publisher, Stonehaven Press

Acknowledgments

This book is a culmination of many years of effort in so many fields of endeavor. No man can successfully accomplish anything meaningful without the help of many around him.

Although I already mentioned my wife on the dedication page, it would be wrong to not list more of what she has done to get this book written and published. First and foremost, she backed my play in pursuing my dream of traveling to dangerous countries as I worked for God. She drove me to the airport for each of my mission trips, prayed for me while I was gone, and picked me up on my return to America. She listened to my endless stories of what I had seen and the people I had met while on my journeys. She backed me up even to the extent of joining me on several of them. Just prior to one of these forays, we were applying for life insurance and were turned down when they heard where we were going. She was undeterred—we made the trip, a difficult one in a hot jungle area with billions of bugs, which she hates. During the writing of this book, she spent countless hours proofreading, making the computer programs work, and offering advice when I was stumped. She never gave up on me or this project. You may have actually read of her in Proverbs 31 (NIV): "Many women do noble things, but you surpass them all. Charm is deceptive, and beauty is fleeting; but a woman who fears the LORD is to be praised."

Thank you to Ron Kingham for being God's answer to getting this published. After realizing I would never agree to jump through the hoops of traditional publishers, I somehow knew that God Himself would provide (with the example of Genesis 22:8). I waited patiently for the Lord to bring it to fruition and in the first few minutes after meeting you, I knew beyond the shadow of any doubt that He had. Your patience with my "street language" as I wrote and your erudite guidance in all things related to publishing were priceless beyond description. As wonderful as all that has been, our new friendship is even more meaningful to me.

Thank you to Cheryl "Coco" Tomlinson, who spent decades praying for me to return to God. Then during my time of desperation, she sent out an emergency email to a long list of prayer warriors. Their prayers rang the halls of heaven, saving my life and resulting in the ministries which have followed. I can't believe you stuck it out so long for me, "my vintage friend."

Thank you to Steve Barkley for always believing in me and for all you did to push me into writing this memoir. It worked, finally. I just had to wait until God changed my calling from traveling for Him to writing for Him. Thank you also for your friendship since I was nineteen-years-old.

Thank you to Jerry DiGiacomo, my first editor who taught me much about writing technique, grammar, and punctuation. Thank you also for your friendship, and your smile, for so many decades.

Thank you to Arlene Hendriks for your expert help in the final proofreading.

Thank you to Kendy Pearson for taking a newbie writer under your wing by email and teaching me so much.

Last in line, but first in my heart, thank you to the many who will never see this page. They will not see it because they are in prison or living in areas where there is no electricity. They are the children of the Living God, who serve Him with their whole hearts under severe persecution all over the world. You have all taught me much that I will need to know during the times to come here in America.

Prologue

"...the LORD had prepared a great fish..." Jonah 1:17 (NKJV)

This fish wasn't like any of the other fish in the sea. Contrary to what many believe, the Bible doesn't say it was a whale, just a very large fish. It was so big it could swallow a prophet whole without hurting him, no chewing involved. We don't know much about it other than that, but we can surmise a few things, knowing the nature of God and how He works. Since God never gets in a hurry, He may have taken a hundred years or more to slowly grow and transform this fish from what it had been when it hatched to what it would be when the time came for it to live out its calling. Then He sent it right where it needed to be, at exactly the right time. He left nothing to chance. He never does.

This verse perfectly describes the course of my life. God spent fifty years transforming and preparing me to live out my calling. Then, when the time came, He sent me right where I needed to be, at exactly the right time. He left nothing to chance. He never does.

1

A Bad Idea

It's a well-known principle of rock climbing that every route looks easy from the ground. From that angle, there are millions of handholds and footholds all the way up to the top. Then when you begin the climb, they all vanish. They evidently pull back inside the rock, leaving the climber to search frantically for any tiny outcropping which might possibly hold his or her weight.

I first encountered this phenomenon on the eastern side of the Sierra Nevada mountains, not far from Yosemite National Park, the epitome of climbing in America. I was at a family gathering near the foot of those beautiful mountains. My uncle lived in a mobile home on a piece of land there. One day, two of my cousins decided to stroll with me over to a nearby three-hundred-foot cliff which went straight up, as I looked at it from the front. On each side, a half-mile hike led around and up to the top. That was for flatlanders, not for me. My expensive rock-climbing shoes were at home, three hundred miles away, since I hadn't expected to do any climbing on this family weekend. But I wasn't going to let that deter me. I could make my motorcycle boots work since I could see there were a plethora of easy footholds all the way up. On a normal climb, I'd have a partner and ropes with all the technical gear, such as wedges and carabiners, to make it safe. But this was a walk in the park. I wouldn't need any equipment today.

I was in the best shape of my life, so I told my cousins I'd meet them at the top. They began walking up and around as I headed straight up the granite face. The first one hundred fifty feet were as easy as it had looked from below. There were indeed good handholds and wide ledges where I could rest as I scanned above to make sure I was taking a workable route. At first, it wasn't much different from climbing a ladder—plenty to hold on to and wide footholds. Then it began to get harder, and a small pinch of worry began to tug at the back of my mind. This might not have been the best idea I ever had. But going back down is always harder than going up, so that wasn't an option. I kept moving up, hoping I was at the worst part. Maybe it would get easier as I went on like it had seemed when I looked up from the ground. But instead of getting easier, the handholds got smaller and more difficult so only two or three of my fingers could fit, and the footholds were just as bad.

I came to a place where I wondered if I could make it any farther at all. I took some time studying it, and I really began to worry. I thought of that adage about things looking so easy from the ground.

The climbing was tough here, but I had no choice other than to make it work. I was right at the limit of my amateur ability. It was taking all my strength to move up at all, and I was getting pretty worn out. I was glad it was only a three-hundred-foot route. If it were longer, I'd have been in real trouble, with the level of energy it was taking from me now. I kept moving up the only route I could find.

Finally, at around two hundred feet, I reached a small "ledge" which was two inches wide, only enough for the sides of my feet, not enough to give me a rest. There were no reachable handholds at all. I stretched my left hand upward as far as I could. The next good handhold was still about three feet above that point. Now I was in major trouble. It was taking all my strength to keep my feet on this tiny ledge, and my strength was quickly running out. If I were to reach the good hold above, I'd have to find a way to lunge for it. But to do that, I'd need a good foothold as a base from which to make the lunge, and there were no footholds at all.

I thought seriously for the first time about trying to down-climb, but as I looked below my feet, all the holds I had used to get up here had disappeared and I knew I had no chance of finding them again. I tried to ignore the view of the ground below as it seemed to want to suck me back down into an abyss. That was a sure way to become a news article ("Beginner rock climber falls to his death. No safety equipment was being used at the time."). Only a handful of the best climbers in the world can down-climb safely. I wasn't one of them.

It's interesting how our standards change depending on the "dire-ness meter rating" of our circumstances. When I had pulled myself onto this two-inch ledge, my standards for usable holds were something like "a half-inch outcropping onto which I could get two fingers" and the same thing for a foothold. Now I spotted a tiny crystal in the granite, the size of the lead on a Number Two pencil that needs to be sharpened. It was about thirty inches above where my feet were beginning to tremble from the strain. Sticking out from the rock face about an eighth of an inch, it didn't even resemble a usable foothold. But as I scanned the face of the rock around me, there was nothing else quite as good, either. So, as bad as it was, it was my only option for a foothold. As I looked above me, I found another crystal roughly the same size, just about the height where I could reach it and use it as a one-finger hold for my right hand. I would have to lunge for the ledge above with my left hand…in the unlikely event that my one-finger handhold and my barely perceptible foothold didn't slip off when I put weight on them. I had tried using holds this tiny before, at ground level while practicing, but had never had any success. Only world-class climbers can use crystals so small with any degree of success, and I had only been climbing for a few months. No, I was going to die here. I had been stupid to think I could do this, and this was where my stupidity would reap its natural consequences.

In desperation, my mind raced, trying to think of some other way out of this. I thought of calling to my cousins for help, but there were two problems. One, they were around the back of this massive rock, hiking to the top, and there was no way they could hear me from that far away. Two, even if they did, it would be a thirty-minute round trip run down to our uncle's place and back with a rope for me. The way my feet were beginning to tremble from fatigue, I was about to peel off the tiny ledge within seconds.

I had less than a minute to live. If I waited any longer, I wouldn't have the strength to make my desperation move.

Knowing that I was 99% likely to die trying this, but 100% likely to die if I did nothing, I lunged upward with my right motorcycle boot on that tiny crystal and one finger of my right hand pulling hard on the other rock crystal above. I strained upward as high as I could with my left hand. Against all the laws of physics, my holds held firm as I lunged. I caught the ledge above. Hanging by that left hand, I brought my right hand up and got a good grip, did a pull-up, then muscled my way up to get my torso onto the ledge. I then pulled the rest of me up so I could get one foot on it, and used that foot to push with as I stood up. I had done the impossible and survived. I stood there for a while on that one-foot-wide ledge regaining my strength and my composure, afraid to look down because death still beckoned from below. As my strength came back and my breathing returned to normal, I examined the rock face above. It looked more like what I had seen from the ground. I cautiously resumed the climb, not wanting to get in a hurry and make a dumb and deadly mistake at this point.

When I reached the top, my cousins were waiting, serenely enjoying the beautiful view of the pine-covered valley below. I never said a word to them about what I had just been through. How do you explain something like that? "As you guys strolled up here, I almost died from my own stupidity." No, better to just keep it to myself.

I couldn't believe my "luck."

2

Genesis of An Adrenaline Junkie

I hadn't been like the other kids. Some may attribute this to my being an only child, but looking back now, I realize it was more than that. It took decades for me to understand how God was creating the spiritual DNA of a wandering adrenaline junkie.

My dad had built a bare-bones stairway in the back of the two-story house. It had a handrail at normal height and another rail at knee height. That left a space between the knee-board and the handrail which allowed me to crawl between them and jump off any particular stair. At the age of six, I decided this must be was how courage was measured. The higher the step I leaped from, the braver I must be. Being an only child, I wasn't competing with anyone else, just my previous best jump. I began about six steps from the bottom, and as the months went by, I got braver and braver, slowly working my way up the stairs. When I got close to the top, I really had to think about how much I wanted to be brave. The thought of broken bones never entered my mind, never having known anyone at that point who had broken an arm or a leg. It was just that my survival instincts were beginning to kick in. Sometimes I'd have to stand on a particular step for a long time, holding onto the outside of the handrail. Finally, I'd gather my courage, remind myself that people didn't die from this (as far as I knew at age six), and then I'd let go and sail through the air, landing in one piece and feeling good about how cool life was. I was definitely going to go places and do things when I grew up, and this was proof.

As I progressed, I'd take time to ready myself for the next step upward. I'd look at it from the ground, then from up on the stairway, safely inside the handrail. Then I'd talk to myself about how it was only a little bit higher than my previous personal best. Over a period of months, I made it all the way up to the second-floor landing. After jumping from there a few times I really took the bull by the horns and stood up on the knee-high rail of the landing and, after some soul-searching, took flight. It was an eye-opener; I hit the ground so hard, my knee flew up and bloodied my lip. I didn't have anyone to explain to me about rolling when I hit, thus absorbing the shock. Being six years old, I never figured it out for myself. I just knew I needed a new hobby, and my stair jumping came to an end.

When I was ten, we moved to a small town in northern California. We lived with forests all around us, and I was in heaven. I now realized I was a forest person, but I had no way of getting out of town and into the woods. My parents weren't hikers, so asking them to go with me was never an option. I never considered it—never even thought of it—until much later in life when I realized other kids went hiking with their folks. I just knew I loved being in the woods and needed to find a way to make it happen. The forest began just a short walk from my front door and beckoned to me every day.

The school bus stop was right in front of my house. Each day I watched from the bus window as we drove out to the main road, turned right and went one mile along the side of the forest, then turned right again and into the school driveway. After weeks of watching and studying, I felt certain I could find a path through the woods and walk to school by myself. If I could make it work, I could get to school on time and still get my fix of being in the woods every day. So, after careful consideration, one morning I hid behind a shed as the other kids got on the bus and watched as it drove away. I then began my adventure, crossing the road, bypassing the few houses, and entering a pine forest about which I knew absolutely nothing; but ten-year-olds just don't really think they might fail in this type of endeavor. Or at least that's how my thought process went. Maybe that's why I wasn't like the other kids. I never really thought about it until decades later when I realized just how strange I had been for doing this kind of thing at all.

I found a path which went in the general direction of my school and followed it. Twice I came to forks in the path and had to stop and consider. This way or that? Hmmm. I had never heard of compasses, nor could I have afforded to buy one if I had. I walked a short distance down one path, then came back and tried the other. Yes, this one felt right. I continued on that one, hoping for the best and thinking that if I didn't find the school at some point, I'd have to backtrack and try the other fork. Fortunately, both my guesses were right, and I came out of the woods with my school in sight. I continued walking to school through the woods like this until we moved away the following summer. I had to live in a city with a school just a few blocks down the street. It seemed so boring after my year of walking to school through the forest every day.

My dad's job was such that we moved somewhere different almost every year. One year we moved twice. I went to four elementary schools, three junior high schools, and three high schools. We never lived in one place long enough for me to put down roots. By the time I graduated, I had the heart of a wanderer. I wanted nothing more than to spend my life continually seeing the new things around the next corner.

My first summer out of high school, I planned on hitch-hiking around the United States. My parents figured something like that was in the making, so for graduation they gave me a three-hundred-dollar car. I was seventeen years old that summer, my first time of being truly on my own. Getting that car made my vagabond plans much easier because I could sleep in the back seat. I didn't need much: just a few blankets to cover myself as I slept, a few changes of clothing, and toiletries. I found that I could get a job in almost any town as a busboy or dishwasher in the restaurants, and I could get free food on top of minimum wage. Gas could be had for nineteen cents per gallon if I looked patiently for it. The most I paid was forty cents per gallon. That summer, I left from California and went as far north as Montana. I stayed put in one city the next winter, then the following summer I went up to Oregon for a few weeks to try to land a job in a lumber mill, just for the adventure. The last thing they wanted in their mills, however, was another Californian, so I set out on the road again, going as far east as Ohio, with some friends sharing my car.

The following winter, I did some soul searching and decided I needed a career path of some kind. None of my ancestors had been to college, so the idea never really appealed to me. My dad was a carpenter, so I became an apprentice, despite having little mechanical ability. I chafed at having to be in one area to learn the trade, but I felt it would come in handy someday.

When I was twenty, I took a couple of weeks off from work and rode a 360 Honda from my home in San Jose, California, to Canada. It was fantastic to be on the road again and to live a dream I had had since I was fifteen, to see how cheaply I could live on the road. That first night my buddy and I pulled our motorcycles into an orchard after dark and covered them with camouflage tarps so nothing would reflect on any passing headlights. We rolled our sleeping bags out on the ground next to our bikes. This was really living. It was a full moon that night, and I lay awake a long time enjoying the beauty of the night sky.

The following night, we were invited to spend the night with a friend I knew who lived in the area where we found ourselves at nightfall. That became the norm for the trip. Either my travel buddy or I knew someone all along the route up to British Columbia. Once in a while, we ran out of friends and my partner insisted we pay money and stay in an official campground. It was only about three dollars each time, but it went against my personal "code of the road" to pay for it when there were a zillion places where we could blend in with the landscape and sleep for free. It was the principle of the thing. But to get along, I acquiesced. As I recall, it only happened twice. I kept a journal of the trip, something I'd never done before. I listed every penny I spent, and during the two-week adventure my expenses added up to a whopping $100.34. That included the ferry over to Vancouver Island and a couple of meals in nice restaurants. Mostly I ate croissants for breakfast, with my lunches being comprised of canned pork and beans.

I had grown up in a Christian home and even attended a Christian school during my last two years of high school. I had become a serious born-again believer at the age of eleven. But at the age of nineteen, I rebelled, thinking I could tell God who was going to be the boss. C. S. Lewis said there are two kinds of people in the world: those who say, "Thy will be done" and those to whom God says, "Okay, have it your way." So, God withdrew from my life and let me have it my way. I never even noticed He was gone. I just knew I loved life and was having a blast. I used the San Francisco Bay Area as a base from which to have my adventures, working just enough so I could afford them.

When I was twenty-two, I spent two months working in a ranch community in South Dakota, helping different ranchers there. I helped feed livestock, brand calves, harvest hay, and whatever else they needed done. I lived in a shack provided by one of the ranchers, sleeping on bales of hay with a twenty-dollar K-Mart sleeping bag thrown over the bales. Fortunately, I had brought along two wool blankets, and they made up for the deficiencies of the cheap sleeping bag. I was comfortable living like that, even when it snowed. When winter set in for real, I floated back to the Bay Area and went back to construction.

In the winter of 1976, I worked on a high rise next to Great America amusement park, helping to build the first Marriott Hotel I ever heard of. I liked the adventure of working ten stories up. Heights scared me and brought an adrenaline rush I came to love.

Many decades later, a pastor friend of mine was doing a sermon series on personality types. He drew a blank when trying to categorize me. In frustration, he told me, "There isn't anyone like you."

3

Motorcycles and Rain

When I first began riding motorcycles, I read a book by Roger Lovin called *The Complete Motorcycle Nomad*. I wanted to travel on my bike, and his book showed me how. I'll never forget one thing he said, "Riding a motorcycle in the rain will provide many interesting stories later, if there is a later."

On my trip to Canada, that phrase came to mind as I rode through a small town in Oregon. The traffic light turned red and I put on the brakes, which had no effect at all. I didn't even slow down as I slid through the intersection. Thankfully, no one else was coming through it at the time.

A few years later, I was riding in the rain on a southern California freeway known as the Grapevine. It's a mountainous highway just north of Los Angeles, four lanes in each direction at that point. I had no choice but to keep going when the rain began, already being three hundred miles from home. I was on a 750 Honda headed downhill on one of the steepest parts of the road when all the lanes of traffic came to a sudden dead stop. By some miracle, I was in a lane with no one immediately in front of me for about one hundred yards, but on each side of me there was a wall formed by the stopped cars. When I saw the traffic ahead was stopped, I locked up both front and rear brakes, going into a skid. Even though there was still a lot of room in front of me, I'd need all the braking time I could get, with the road as rain-slick as it was. Similar to the time in Oregon, my speed didn't change at all. I was still hydroplaning down the Grapevine at seventy miles per hour. Knowing the habits of southern California drivers, I knew I was seconds away from one of them getting impatient at the delay and thinking, "Hey, that lane next to me has no one in it, I think I'll change into it and make some progress." Then I would die. Miraculously, none of them did it. My mind was racing, but I was already doing everything I could. This was out of my control. I focused on keeping balanced so the motorcycle didn't drift away from the middle of the lane, but all I could really do was watch that stopped car in front of me keep getting closer, very quickly. My speed diminished microscopically while I continued hurtling down the open lane. I gave a brief thought to trying to jump upward just as my motorcycle hit the trunk of the car ahead, so I'd fly over the first car, only hitting the third or fourth one beyond. I didn't know if it would really help anything, and there wasn't time to think it through. Then I saw something that made my heart leap in hope. The cars up ahead were beginning to move. There might be a chance yet. Even if I could just hit that car less hard because it was moving, it would be better than what I had been facing. Finally, I saw the car in front of me move forward as traffic began going again. They were accelerating more slowly than I needed, but they were gaining in speed. In what seemed like slow motion freeze frame, I slid to within a foot of the bumper just as he reached a speed which got him out of my danger zone. I was able to let off the brakes and resume normal riding. My adrenaline was spurting out of my pores. I was going to live! The whole sequence of events had been almost like someone was orchestrating it....

Another time, I was in Midland, Texas, for a family reunion. My favorite cousin had moved three hundred fifty miles away to Waco. He wouldn't be arriving at the reunion until Saturday night, and this was only Wednesday. My uncle had a 750 Honda, and he urged me to take it, go spend a few days with Danny in Waco, then come back with him to Midland for the weekend. I thought that was a great idea, so I borrowed his motorcycle and headed east on a bright sunny May day.

As I rode east, the weather was beautiful for the first fifty miles, then I rode into a hailstorm. It was just one cloud, but the cloud was right over the interstate, right in my way. My uncle's helmet had no face shield, and his windshield was the "café racer" type, which meant I had to bend over and put my face right behind it to block the small hailstones. It was a miserable position, bent over like that, so as soon as I got to an overpass, I stopped and parked under it to wait out the storm. About half an hour went by. The storm moved on, so I got back on the bike...and rode right back into the hailstorm. Once again, I stopped under an overpass and waited. The storm slowly moved on, right along the route I had to take. After another half hour, I got on the Honda again, and sure enough, within a few minutes was right back into the hailstones again, bent over behind the café windshield.

I was irritated, but I wasn't about to let this little cloudburst beat me. It looked pretty small, so I decided my best bet was to just kick up the speed and get to the far side of it. I'd have smooth sailing for the rest of the journey. I sped up to eighty-five miles per hour, just about as fast as I felt comfortable going on a motorcycle. You never know when the front tire might hit a nail, and then I'd be in serious trouble. I didn't ride as fast as a lot of people I knew.

The hail frequently turned to rain, then back to hail again. Then lightning started up and continued intermittently for the whole trip. Sometimes the lightning strike was so close the thunder felt like a blow hitting me. Then the wind picked up worse than anything I had ever ridden through before. Due to the intense rain and hail, visibility dropped to the point I could no longer see the far side of the cloud. I figured I'd just outlast it, and the clear weather on the far side would be worth the trouble of going so fast on a dangerously slick road.

A sudden wind hit me unexpectedly from the right side, sliding me into the other lane and scaring the daylights out of me. I got back into the right-hand lane immediately, hugging as far right as I could. This happened again, and again, and again, until I began hugging the edge of the pavement on the right side of the freeway, so I'd have as much time as possible to react as I slid all the way across the road to the left. I lost count of how many times the wind hit me from that side, always the same side. Each time, it hit so hard it would slide the whole five hundred fifty-pound motorcycle hard to the left, all the way across both lanes of the interstate, within an inch of the edge of the pavement on the left. I kept thinking if it had hit me a few ounces harder, I'd have hit the dirt (mud by now) in the median and I probably would have wiped out, not a fun thought at high speed. Each time, I couldn't believe I had "dodged another bullet." What were the odds I'd slide the exact amount of pavement from right to left, but not the extra fraction of an inch that would take me down? It was as if it had been measured out for me by something controlling the wind.

I felt fortunate each time it happened that there was never another car in the other lane, so I never got into an accident. It didn't dawn on me until afterward, that I was by now the only person on the road. Later in life, I discovered that's a bad sign. It means all the other drivers know something you don't, and it's a good idea to get off the road and find out what's going on.

I was terrified, and many times thought of stopping and getting a motel, but I was young and didn't have a credit card to my name. In addition, I only had enough cash to pay for my gas to Waco and back, nothing extra at all. Several times, I thought of getting off the freeway and trying to find a church to see if they'd let me spend the night in their lobby, but I was too shy to ask. I kept wondering if there might be anyone I knew in any of the towns along the way, but I couldn't think of a soul. I was terrified the whole time I rode in that storm, but I didn't see any option other than to keep going. There was no point in turning around and going back because I still thought I wasn't far from the end of the worst part.

The lightning continued getting worse, beyond anything I had ever seen. Twice, the strikes were so close the force of them nearly knocked me off the bike. If I had had any options at all, I'd have stopped and waited until the next day to finish the trip. My back had been hurting for hours by now as I had to make this whole ride in the bent-over-forward position to stay behind the tiny windshield to keep my eyes from being hit by the hailstones.

It took more than five hours of this kind of riding, but finally I arrived in Waco just as the rain let up a bit. I followed the directions to my cousin's apartment, parked the motorcycle, and stood up, straightening out the kinks in my back for the first time in ages. When I knocked on the door, he opened it, looked at me in astonishment and said, "I do *not* believe you rode that motorcycle through this tornado!"

My knees got wobbly and I needed to sit down. I had ridden for hours through a tornado which killed three people. I was speechless. In all the hours of this ride, the rain and hail had been so thick, I had never caught sight of the funnel cloud. If I had, I'd have turned around and gone back, no matter what it took. It was at this point it finally dawned on me that I had been the only one on the freeway for much of the trip. Everyone else had heard the warnings on their car radios and taken shelter.

The next day, five more tornadoes circled Waco, and it hailed twelve inches on the road I had ridden over. My dad had urged me to wait until the following day to make the trip. If I had, I might have died.

I couldn't believe my "luck."

4

The Compass

When I was twenty-seven, I set up a trip to the high Sierra Nevada mountains, with the idea of teaching myself how to hunt. I had spent some time looking at a map of the area my hunting buddy and I had picked out where we would camp and hunt. There was a paved road going over the mountains from west to east. At the summit, there was a dirt road going due north from the paved one. The dirt road was nine miles long, at which point it ended with nothing but forest beyond. We figured this would be a great area for deer, since it was on the edge of Golden Trout Wilderness, stretching out for fifty miles north of us. There were no more roads until the far side of the wilderness. That should make for good hunting, we thought.

We set up camp at the end of the nine-mile dirt road. We had the area all to ourselves, surrounded by a thick pine forest and rolling, boulder-strewn terrain. We pitched my friend's two-man dome tent, rolled out the sleeping bags and prepared some backpacking food for dinner. In getting set up for the next day, I got some lunch meat and bread from our cooler and made sandwiches to carry in my daypack. I double checked that I had fire-making materials in one of the pouches and saw to it that my wool vest was in the main compartment, in case it got colder while I was hunting away from camp. I had given a lot of thought to wilderness survival.

The next morning, we were up before the sun. I donned my daypack, pulling the canteen strap over my head and around one shoulder. As we moved out to begin hunting, heavy rain began to fall. My buddy and I went separate ways, planning to meet back at camp later in the day. I walked a short distance, but discouraged by the rain, I turned around and went back to camp. I shrugged off my daypack and put it into the cab of my truck to keep it dry, then found a log to sit on, still wearing my rain poncho.

Before long, I got bored just sitting there, so I decided to get out of camp in the hope of stumbling onto a deer. I wouldn't be gone long, so there was no need to get the daypack out of my truck. Grabbing only my rifle, I walked back south along the dirt road on which we had driven in, the day before. After a few hundred yards, I decided to take a walk out from the road in a perpendicular direction, hoping to spot a buck. I knew there is a tendency to get turned around easily in heavy forest, especially in a rain-storm, so I carefully took my bearings, looking at the road on my left and right. From that point, I walked at a perpendicular angle away from the road and out into the forest. I went what I thought was about three hundred yards, then turned around to go back to the road. I walked...and walked...and walked some more. At some point, I knew beyond any doubt I had walked further back than I had walked out before turning around. Now what? The only thing I could think of was, somebody had stolen the whole road.

How do you steal a road?

I walked and walked. Then I walked some more. At this point, I knew I was lost. I also knew only one direction could get me out, and that was back toward camp, but where was it? The wrong direction would just get me deeper into the Golden Trout Wilderness, north, west, or east. But I had no food, no tent, no sleeping bag, and I figured I wouldn't really make it far on an empty stomach.

At this time of my life, I was an avid rock climber in Yosemite. I had had numerous close calls with death and faced them all calmly. I was proud of the fact that I could keep my cool, even in the knowledge that I would likely be dead in the next minute or two. Not many people can keep their head in this kind of situation, but I could. Now, faced with the certain knowledge that I was lost in the Sierra Nevada mountains, I panicked. With no idea when it began, I realized I was running as fast as I could. A deep recess in my mind said, "This is how people die in the wilderness, running nowhere until they die." So, I forced myself down to a walk, going...where? The same unknown place I had been running to, evidently, just not as fast. As I continued forward, I found myself running again, and had to force myself to slow down again. I went through this cycle several times, then realized I was in serious trouble. I was using up energy I might need desperately before this was over.

I kept walking. I was making progress, but toward safety or away from it? It was stupid to continue this when I might be going the wrong way. I found a shallow overhang to keep the rain off and stood there for a while, thinking my way through this. There was no place to sit without getting wet, but as long as I stood leaning against the overhang, I could rest somewhat, and stay dry.

I went over what I knew for certain: I had driven nine miles due north from an east-to-west paved road, then made camp. How I had gotten lost, I had no idea, but I remembered that no one has a stride which is evenly matched, left leg to right leg. One step will always be slightly and consistently longer than the other. So somehow, I had walked in a semicircle and come around north of where the road came to an end, missing it entirely. Nothing else made sense. So...was I northeast of the road or northwest of it? There was no way to know. How do I get out of this? All I could know for certain was that nine miles south of me (maybe ten by now, after my running in an unknown direction) was a paved road which would lead me back to food, shelter, and television. I took some time to think it over. There was no other way out. I had a long walk ahead of me. I knew it would take at least two days to get this sorted out. It would take me all of this day just to get back to the paved road nine miles away since there were no easy trails. It was just broken, rugged country. Once back on pavement, I'd have to figure out whether to go east or west once I got there. This would take time. The sun would go down at some point and I'd be stuck roughing it somewhere in the woods for the night. The next day after I found the right way to go to get back to the dirt road, it would be another nine-mile walk back to camp. There were no shortcuts. Two days hiking with at least one night spent in the woods, but I had no choice.

My daypack was sitting uselessly back in my truck, wherever that was. I had no food with me, no canteen; just my rifle, my poncho and...a compass. "For some reason," I hadn't put the compass into my pack as I got ready for this hunting trip. I hadn't really given it any thought but had stuck it absently into my pocket and forgotten about it.

Now I took the compass out and checked it, looking at it for the first time since arriving in the Sierras. And now, wouldn't you know it? The darn thing was broken. It showed north to be in the wrong direction. I knew where north was, it was that way, but the compass showed it be the other way. Oh man, I was really depressed. Then the thought came to me: I got into this mess by thinking my own sense of direction was right when circumstances had clearly proved me wrong. Now those same instincts said, "Don't trust this piece of army surplus trash." But as I turned it around this way and that, the needle stayed certain, pointing to a consistent direction. Did I dare trust something other than my own instincts? It was the hardest thing I had ever done, but I put the compass back into my pocket and set out in the direction it had shown to be south. The rain was heavier than ever, and I walked with my head down, the poncho's hood over my head limiting my vision as I worked my way left and right around trees and boulders but heading in the way the compass had shown.

After a hundred yards or so, I wondered if I should double check my direction. My mind said, "Nah, only city folks would worry about that. I'm an outdoorsman, I know I'm headed in the right direction." The thought came to me next was: "Yeah…isn't that how I got into this mess, by trusting my own internal compass?" I wrestled with myself for several minutes, not wanting to waste time digging it back out of my pocket and out from under the poncho, but I finally decided double checking myself wasn't an entirely bad idea, so I did. To my shock, I discovered that in the one hundred yards I had made a complete one-hundred-eighty-degree turn and was headed right back into the Golden Trout Wilderness. So, for the rest of the adventure, I walked with the compass in my hand, checking it every fifty yards, and after about half an hour, much to my amazement, I walked straight back into my camp. If I had missed it by one hundred yards east or west, I'd have had that long two-day walk ahead of me. As it turned out it couldn't have been any more perfect if God had been directing me the whole time….

The odds against me walking in circles all morning, then all the way back through the woods and hitting my camp without having to do that nine-mile trek in both directions were beyond calculation. Wow, what incredible "luck."

But in this instance, I needed even more "luck." That night, after we crawled into our sleeping bags inside our tent, it began to snow. We didn't know how much snow was expected, but we knew we were at a high elevation. We each had four-wheel-drive vehicles, but if the snow gets deep enough, even those can get stranded. I got more and more nervous. I wanted to get out while we could, but my buddy wanted to stay and keep hunting. We argued over it, with me finally making him miserable enough that he agreed our hunt was over for this year. We packed up and left. We found out later that storm after storm brought more than six feet of snow to the area, snow which didn't melt until the following spring. If I had been lost in the woods up there while trying to hike out, I would have died. My flannel shirt and rain poncho wouldn't have been enough to keep me alive even one night in the snow. My life was saved by that compass. On top of which, if we hadn't called off the hunt and gotten out, they'd have found our bodies in the spring.

I couldn't believe my "luck." Twice.

5

Royal Arches Epic

We had been climbing in Yosemite Valley for two weeks, camping on the valley floor at night. My climbing partner, Jason, and I began each day by looking above as the melting snow turned into a flowing stream which cascaded over the face of the climb known as Royal Arches. I badly wanted to do that climb because it went up to 1,100 feet, more than twice the height I had ever climbed before. Among its many features, the final pitch was a friction slab, which meant there were no handholds or footholds. The steepness of the rock at that point was low enough so it could be climbed by using the friction between the rock and the soles of our shoes. Climbers have to rely on technical rock-climbing shoes with synthetic soles which grip the tiny crystals in the granite far better than street shoes could do. As a matter of fact, wearing street shoes on a friction face was a guarantee of failure, since shoe leather isn't able to grip granite crystals. Given that friction is the key on this type of climbing, the route has to be absolutely bone-dry. Any moisture will render the specialized climbing shoes slippery and useless. The friction slab on this particular climb was right at the top, so a misstep at that altitude could be fatal. In fact, one of the most famous Yosemite rock climbers had been killed in a fall from that very climb not long before, because he underestimated the danger.

As we began each day looking up hopefully, the Royal Arches climb still had a shallow waterfall over its entire face, so we had to settle for shorter and less spectacular climbs. We did climbs called Bishop's Terrace, Harry Daley, and the Nutcracker. The month was May, and the snow above had been melting steadily for several weeks. We began to notice that each day the water flowing over Royal Arches was visibly less than the day before, and by the second week, we could see dry patches on the friction slab above. They got larger and larger, day by day, until we felt we could safely make the climb by simply stepping over the rivulets as we came to them.

Jason had done this climb before and knew the route. One of the cool things about the Arches was that when you reached the top, you didn't have to rappel back down the same route you went up. You could hike down the back on a trail which Jason knew. Rappelling is fun, but you have to leave some of your gear behind (a carabiner or a nylon strap) since something has to be there to hold your rope for the rappel. Once you are down, a piece of your gear is still up there wedged into a crack or hanging from a bolt someone else had installed into the rock. Rappelling can get expensive over time, with a piece of equipment left behind each time, never to be recovered.

We had been camping next to two college students from Colorado who were getting to live their dream of climbing in Yosemite. Each morning we wished each other well, and each evening we swapped stories of our exploits. Jason was a lot more experienced than I, and it seemed the Colorado guys were even more experienced than him. I was in good company.

One evening we talked it over, deciding it was now dry enough to safely climb the Arches. The Colorado guys decided to join us, as this would be a great opportunity for them to make such a classic ascent. Jason said there was no need to leave at the crack of dawn, since his memory was that it was only a two-hour climb. We could have a leisurely morning, then begin the climb at eleven o'clock. Much later, I found out it's a good idea to plan for seven hours minimum for Royal Arches, with ten hours being more realistic. We were in for quite an adventure due to leaving that late in the day.

I was older than the other climbers and had been around a good bit, hunting in snow-covered mountains and traveling the country on a motorcycle in all kinds of weather. For this climb, I took a day pack with several candy bars and a water bottle, even though it was supposed to be a short climb, hours-wise. I also put a hoodie sweatshirt into the day pack, since snow still covered a lot of the peaks. The day was warm, but Yosemite weather can change quickly. When it comes to safety equipment and supplies, I always feel it's better to have it and not need it than to need it and not have it. The other three climbers made no provision for any unexpected eventualities. Oh well, I figured, that was their choice.

We climbed in two teams. Jason and I were roped together, while the Colorado guys partnered up the same way. We took the lead, the Colorados following us up the route. As Jason climbed, he stopped every ten to fifteen feet and placed a wedge firmly into a crack in the granite, then put a carabiner through the industrial-strength wire loop which was built into the wedge. Then he put his rope into the carabiner via a one-way gate in its oval design (this part of climbing is called "placing protection," which climbers have shortened to "placing pro"). That way if he fell, the distance he could fall was limited by the rope, wedge, and carabiner combination. I would be tied into the other end of the rope, holding it firmly to limit how far he could fall. When he reached a place close to the end of our one-hundred-sixty-five-foot rope, he'd "place pro" into three cracks in the rock, then put his rope through each of the respective carabiners. At that point, he'd be safely anchored to the rock (this is called a "belay position") so he could hold the rope for me as I climbed up from below. As I climbed, he would take up the slack in the rope so if I slipped, I wouldn't fall too far before he caught me. As I climbed, I removed all the wedges which he had put into the cracks as he led the way up (this task is known as "cleaning the route"). Once I got up to where he was, I gave him back all the gear I had collected, then clipped into his belay so I could protect him as he unclipped and moved on upward. In this way, we moved up each rope length (called a "pitch") similar to the way an inchworm moves.

Royal Arches is a pretty easy climb, for the most part. There are easy hand- and foot-holds for most of its eleven-hundred-foot climb, and plenty of places to rest and catch your breath. As I looked down, I could see the Colorado guys were climbing well, coming up behind us.

We weren't going as fast as I had expected, but we made steady progress. About halfway up, we moved sideways through a small waterfall. Each of us had to be careful to plan where we placed our feet so the soles of our shoes stayed dry. All of us made it through with no trouble and we continued upward.

One of the most famous parts of this climb was the "Rotten Log." Many hundreds of feet up into the climb, there is a large crevice, hundreds of feet deep, blocking the route. It is possible to cross only because, at some point in the distant past, a tree had fallen from above and had wedged horizontally into the crevice, forming a bridge right where it was needed for this climb to be possible. The climber has to cross this log to the other side in order to continue the route.

I set up a belay position and fed the rope out as Jason walked across it, like an ironworker on a skyscraper construction project. Not me. After Jason set up a belay on the far side, I straddled it like a horse and inched my way across. The drop of several hundred feet seemed to be pulling me down. I tried to stay focused on my destination, the rock face waiting for me on the other end of the log. It only took a few minutes to get across, and I breathed a sigh of relief to have solid granite under my shoes again. We moved on up as the Colorado guys followed behind us across the log.

This was taking a lot longer than Jason had planned, and the sun was getting low on the horizon when we reached the friction traverse near the top of the climb. "Traverse" means the climber doesn't go up or down, but sideways across the rock. In this case, we would traverse to the left, finally reaching what they call "the jungle," actually just some pine trees which make for a solid belay point. There were three problems here. One, there was water cascading over it. Two, being a friction slab, there were no cracks except for one at the halfway point in this traverse. As I belayed Jason, if he slipped on wet rock, he'd have a bad time of it since he would fall in a kind of bouncing pendulum with me holding his rope until he reached a point exactly below me, at which time he would climb back up to me and we'd start over again. If that happened, we could only hope he wouldn't break any bones as he bounced across the granite before coming to a stop. The third problem was that those trees looked to be a long way from us, maybe farther than our rope could reach. There was no way to know for sure, but our only choice was to keep going and hope for the best.

With me set up in a secure belay position, Jason moved out, going carefully and picking his route where he could see patches of dry granite between the streams of cascading water. I was glad we hadn't tried this even three days earlier. If we had, I think we'd have run into too much water to safely proceed and been stuck on the rock face with no way up. Watching Jason move, I could tell he was nervous. The Colorado climbers came up behind me, and together we watched the drama unfold as the sun set behind the mountains. After what seemed like an eternity, Jason reached the crack in the rock at the halfway point of the traverse. He took a wedge from his gear strap and set it firmly in place and clipped into it. He called over to us, "Whew. Now I feel better." We felt better too, and Jason continued moving crablike to the left toward "the jungle." I looked at the amount of rope left in front of me and realized it was going to be close. He could move faster now, as the rock surface ahead of him was dry for the rest of the way. When he got about fifteen feet from the jungle, I ran out of rope.

I called out to him, "That's all the rope you've got." I had never run into this before and wasn't sure what we'd do now, but there was really only one option.

He called back to me, "You're going to have to undo the belay and move sideways with me." I didn't like this at all. Neither of us would be belaying the other. We'd both be traversing at the same time. If either of us fell, which was a strong possibility, he would pull the other off balance and both of us would fall. The one saving grace was that the wedge in the middle would hold solid to protect us, so the worst that could happen would be that we would both pendulum until we finally came to rest below the wedge, a bit banged up, but alive. As I thought it over, I knew there was no other choice, so I began unclipping the carabiners, jerking the wedges upward and out of the crack where they'd been, then stashing them on the web belt around my neck.

When I finished cleaning the belay position of all our equipment, I called over to Jason and we both began cautiously moving sideways to the left. It was tricky work, me stepping carefully to avoid the water on the rock, Jason taking a step, then looking back across at me to make sure there was enough slack in the rope to keep each of us from pulling the other off balance. The first goal was to get Jason into the trees where he could set up a belay. He was only fifteen feet from it as we began this part, but that seemed like a long way at the moment. In the meantime, I had to focus on my part: scan the rock for a dry spot, step carefully onto it, all the while keeping perfect balance. It was crucial that I examine the area for each step to make sure there were others past that one, to avoid boxing myself into a totally wet area and having to backtrack. There were no handholds on this slab, it was all footwork. Plan the next move, execute it, look at my partner to make sure all was well. The fear factor was high, but I kept comforting myself by thinking about the wedge Jason had placed into the crack between us and putting all my confidence in it. If we fell, that would keep us alive.

Finally, he called over, "Okay, hold where you are, I'm at the trees." I froze in place and watched as he put a strap around a tree trunk and tied into it. "Okay, you're on belay."

After a heartfelt sigh of relief, I continued carefully working my way toward the wedge in the middle, the wedge on which we were trusting our lives. When I had gone a few more feet, Jason told me to stop so he could belay to two more trees, a good insurance policy against Murphy's Law. Once he had his belay point in place, I continued the traverse. When I finally reached the wedge in the middle, my heart nearly stopped. There it was, dangling loosely in the crack. It had pulled loose sometime after Jason had placed it into the crack. It had been worthless all this time. As we had traversed together, trusting the wedge to save us if we fell, it had been bouncing around loose in the crack, absolutely useless.

I called over to Jason, "Look at this." I held up the rope for him to see our protection there, anchored in nothing but air.

All he could say was, "Aw man…." Both of us were nauseated at the thought of what might have happened.

From there, the rest of the traverse was easy. I had moved past the cascading water and now I only moved slowly enough so my partner could take up the slack in the rope as I got closer. Soon I was into the trees myself. Looking back, we could see the Colorado climbers coming close behind us.

The sun was going down and dark, heavy clouds were moving in. There was no time to lose, so we moved up to the top of the pine-covered area. There was one last short pitch to climb, where the trees stopped and the bare rock began again. It wasn't far, but it was just tricky enough, so we still had to use the gear for safety. We hurriedly set up a belay and Jason began climbing upward as I fed out the rope behind him. In a few minutes, he was at the top, then he belayed me. The Colorados were still close behind us.

When I reached the top, Jason took the belay apart, coiled the one hundred sixty-five-foot rope and slung it over his shoulder.

Then we waited for the others to catch up. Since the way down was a hike of several hours on a back trail and Jason was the only one who knew the way, we had to wait until we were all together before proceeding or the Colorados would get lost in the encroaching darkness.

By the time they caught up and coiled their rope, it was almost fully dark. Jason still thought he could find the way in the semidarkness, so he led out. The Colorados went next and I brought up the rear. There was a reason for this: I wasn't going to share my food. We hadn't eaten since breakfast and we were all hungry. As I brought up the rear, I took off my pack, unzipped it quietly, then pulled out and donned the hoodie. I ate the first of the candy bars, staying far enough back so no one would notice that I had food. I felt no guilt at all about not sharing my snacks. If we couldn't find the trail and get down in the dark, we'd have to spend the night up here. And if it began snowing, which was entirely possible at the altitude, we'd be in a survival situation before morning. Hypothermia kills, and even with my hoodie and a few candy bars, it would be touch and go. I felt no compunctions at all. I had prepared, and they hadn't. This was during the B.C. days (Before Christ), and I had no humanitarian feelings when it came to surviving versus dying because the others hadn't thought it through. It would be sad if they died, but I could always find new climbing partners.

We were walking steadily downhill in the darkness. It was tricky, knowing a misstep could send one of us falling to a nasty death. I wondered how Jason could see where he was going. As it turned out, he was wondering also. Frequently, he'd stop, and we'd have to wait for a cloud to move out of the way so the dim starlight could give him some idea of where we were. Then we'd get as far as we could before the next cloud came over again. This was getting a bit scary.

Then, in one of those times of brief starlight, we came to the end of the trail. Jason stopped abruptly and we all gathered around him. We were at the top of a cliff with no way down. We couldn't see anything below in the dim light, but this was clearly not the path Jason had been looking for.

"So, what now?" I asked him.

"I don't know," he replied. He scanned the rocks around, looking for clues, as the Colorados and I exchanged worried looks.

He led back the way we had come and found what he thought was the trail. At least it did lead downward. We took that "trail" as far as we could and ended up at the top of another cliff. By now it was obvious that he was lost, which meant we were all lost. Everyone began offering opinions and tempers ran short. None of them had eaten since breakfast and they were feeling it. So was I, just not as badly as them.

I lost track of how many dead ends we reached, only to have to backtrack and look for another route. It went on for hours. The clouds got thicker, and the periods of starlight got farther and farther between until they stopped altogether. It was now totally overcast and dark. None of us had thought to bring flashlights (note to self: next time bring one in my daypack, no matter how simple and easy the climb looks). The only comfort was, we could tell we were getting lower in elevation each time we came to a dead end. We would turn back, stumble along until we found a promising semi-trail and follow it downward, only to reach another impasse. We couldn't tell how low we were getting, though, because once the starlight was gone for good, it was only slightly less than pitch black. We could see each other dimly and we could see our immediate surroundings, but not well.

It was getting colder and colder. I surreptitiously ate another candy bar but was still hungry. I knew the others were having it even rougher. And I was getting worried that it would start snowing any minute.

Finally, I took the bull by the horns. "We need to set up a rappel and begin inching our way down the rock face." There was a stunned silence. I couldn't see the others' faces in the darkness, but I could feel their astonishment. I knew they were thinking I must have lost my mind.

The older of the two Colorado guys, Steve, finally spoke up. "In the dark? That would be suicide."

"It'll be suicide to stay here all night if it starts snowing," I retorted. "And by then it'll be too late to try what I'm suggesting."

"How are you going to set it up in this darkness?" he asked.

"I can see well enough right in front of me to at least find a tree. I'll set it up using the tree as the rappel anchor, then I'll go first, going down until I find a ledge large enough for us all. Then I'll call to you, and you'll all follow me, then we'll pull the ropes down and set it up again. We can do that, step by step, all the way down." I had been thinking about this for a while now, and it seemed like a good plan.

"What if you can't find a ledge big enough for us all? Or what if you end up hanging in space where you can't reach the rock face? What then?"

"Then I'll 'batman' back up and try again somewhere else." The term "batman" meant to climb up a rope, in climber jargon.

"You won't be able to climb back up the whole one hundred sixty-five feet of rope. Your arms will get tired and you'll fall to your death." This guy was a ray of sunshine.

"I carry a Prusik with me, around my neck." I held it up where he could see it or could have if it hadn't been so dark. Anyway, he could see I was holding something up, which he could take my word for as being a Prusik. A Prusik is a short loop of thin rope which can be used to climb up a rope. It acts somewhat like a "ratchet for ropes." You wrap it around the rope you are going to climb and connect it to your harness. It will slide easily up the rope you are climbing, but if you put your weight on it (meaning if you fall, or even just want to rest), it tightens up so you don't slide back down the main rope. I had learned about the technique in Yosemite mountaineering school and immediately saw that it could be a lifesaver, so it was one of the first pieces of equipment I bought. It seemed likely Steve had never heard of a Prusik before, despite his longer experience in climbing.

There was a long silence as we all thought about it. Steve's partner said nothing. Jason's attitude to everyone around him was to let them take any chance they wanted to take. I heard him say once, "If you fall through stupidity, it's your emergency, not mine." We climbed together, but we weren't close. He finally spoke to Steve, saying, "If he wants to do it, let him do it." He handed me his coiled rope.

To set up a rappel, you first pick a strong place for a base. Usually, there's a bolt fastened into the rock by a previous climber, and all subsequent climbers use that bolt. You have to clip a carabiner to the bolt and run your rope through the carabiner until you get to the halfway point of the rope. At that point, as it hangs down, it's the same length on both sides. That means for a rope length of the standard one hundred sixty-five feet, you have eighty-two-and a-half feet for your rappel. You can't use all that length, though, because you have to use some of it to clip into your harness, taking some of its length which gets deducted from what you have hanging down for the rappel. You also have to leave a few extra feet because as the rope goes between your legs, you have one hand holding tightly to it below you, wrapped around your leg for extra friction. This "braking hand" controls your rate of descent as the rope slides through it and can even stop your rappel if that's what you want to do, just by gripping it tightly, like putting on the brakes.

In our case, using a bolt was not an option because we were no longer at the top of any climb, but somewhere far off the track. There were no bolts. In this case, the only option was to use trees for our rappel anchor. They needed to be big enough to hold us but small enough so that we wouldn't use up unnecessary footage of rope going around it, rope which we would need to get as far as possible down the rock. And since I'd be rappelling in almost complete darkness, I wanted to tie both of our ropes together, ours with the Colorados' rope, giving me close to one hundred sixty-five feet of options as I looked for another rappel point, where we could set up for the next leg of the journey down. Having two ropes of one hundred sixty-five feet gave me twice as much chance of finding a suitable ledge where we could all tie in. And with heavy clouds moving in, I didn't consider this to be optional. This could be life or death before morning.

Now we came to the heart of the matter. This was going to be tense, I knew. "I'm going to need your rope, Steve. If I'm going to make this work, I need the full one hundred sixty-five feet of opportunity given by having two ropes. So, I need your rope to tie into mine."

"No. You'll end up rappelling off the end of the rope and falling to your death. I won't be a party to your death."

"I'm not that stupid, Steve. I'll go slow, feeling my way, and I'll be holding the rope below me with my braking hand. I'll probably find a place for us to set up before I run out of rope, but if not, I'll realize I'm close to the end and I'll 'batman' back up and find another point and try again."

He was angry, I knew, but so was I. No one is stupid enough to rappel blindly off the end of their rope. That was shallow thinking on his part.

I waited a minute as he thought, but I was quickly running out of patience. I wanted to get going on this, and I didn't need him trying to babysit me.

Finally, I was done being nice. In my B.C. days, violence was my default answer to every problem. And when I was angry like now, violence seemed to radiate out of me. I had seen it in myself before.

At times like this, I scared people just by looking at them. And it was worse now because we were in serious trouble, and I was offering to do something about it. I wasn't going to let this lily-livered college kid keep me up on this rock all night.

"Give me your rope." He stood there in the dark, not moving a muscle. I waited, then I took a quick step toward him, snarling, "Give me the rope." Every molecule of my body was vibrating menace. I never believed in threatening, if violence is imminent. It's not good to give your opponent a chance to set up to defend against you. At this point, I was done asking; the seconds were ticking down. I wasn't going to ask again; I was just going to knock him out and take the rope. He'd end up having to make the rappel while nursing a broken nose, but that would be what he had chosen for himself. After several tension-filled seconds, he slammed the coil of rope into my shoulder. I didn't care, the important thing was that I had it and could now begin setting up the rappel.

With both ropes coiled over my shoulder I moved down the slope and walked carefully along the top of the cliff, peering into the darkness for a suitable tree. The first few were either too small or too big, but finally, I found one a couple of feet from the sloped cliff edge and began uncoiling the ropes. I crawled around below it, then took Steve's rope in my left hand and reached up around the tree, pulling it down with my right hand. I tied the end into a loose figure-eight knot. Then, taking Jason's rope, I ran it in reverse, back into the figure-eight knot in Steve's rope, doing what's called a "follow through" with his, so that mine and his were tied together into the same figure-eight. This is the most commonly used climbing knot. It's secure but also can easily be untied when you're done with a climb. The knots can't be jammed up tightly enough to be a problem.

As I got ready to cast the working ends of the ropes down into the darkness below, something sounded a warning in my mind. I couldn't define it, but somehow, I knew beyond the shadow of any doubt that something was drastically wrong here. I went over the knots again in the darkness, feeling them with my hands, and there was nothing wrong there. As I sat there trying to figure out what was going on, and why I felt such danger, the only thing I could think of was that something was wrong with the tree. That didn't make sense either, but I scooted up close and ran my hands up and down it, feeling the side closest to me in the dark, searching for something wrong, a safety check by Braille. Nothing. Then I reached around behind the tree and got a major shock. This was just a rotted out old tree trunk. There was nothing left but thin bark standing upright. If I had put my weight into it, it would have pulled apart like tissue paper, and I'd have plunged to my death on the valley floor below.

I knew the other guys would freak if they knew how close to disaster I had come, so I said nothing. I just untied the ropes from each other and moved a few feet away to the next tree. I ran my hands around it and rapped my knuckles on it hard. It was solid. It was a living, healthy tree with pine needles on its branches. I began tying the ropes together again.

"What are you doing?" came the question from above, I couldn't tell from whom. They knew it shouldn't have taken this long.

"I'm just double checking everything. This is dicey enough without me getting in a hurry." I finished setting up the ropes, then tossed the working ends down into the darkness below.

I clipped the rope into the carabiners on my harness. "All set, I'm heading down," I called to the guys up above. I began walking slowly backwards, over the edge and downward, my left hand on the rope above for balance while my right hand, the braking hand, was below me slowly feeding the rope through, my grip controlling the rate of my descent. I went slowly, picking my way in the dark, step by step walking backwards down the rock. I couldn't see the valley floor below me, so I didn't know how many times we'd have to do this—like an inchworm crawling down the rock face—before we got down. I felt good that at least we were taking steps to get down, rather than having to sit up there all night just hoping it wouldn't snow.

Looking up, I could no longer see the tree which was anchoring my rappel, so it was hard to estimate how far down I had come. It felt like I had come far enough so that when I found a ledge about twelve inches wide which was long enough to accommodate all four of us, I stopped and set up some wedges into a convenient crack, then clipped my harness into the wedge cables. Unclipping myself from the rappel rope, I called up to the others.

"I've found a decent ledge. One of you come on down."

I felt the rope move as one of them clipped into it, then I heard Jason say, "Coming down."

The rope danced back and forth beside me as he moved. In a few minutes, I could make out his figure in the darkness. When he got down to my level, he was ten feet to the left of me as I faced the rock. He was going to miss the ledge.

"Over here," I called. "There's plenty of room." But he didn't move toward me, just kept looking down. I couldn't figure out what he was doing. I said again, "Over here. Tie in so the next guy can come down."

"Just a minute," he said. He stayed there looking down for another long moment. Then he rappelled down out of my sight into the darkness below. I couldn't figure out what he was doing. After several minutes of my wondering what was going on, he called up to me, "I'm standing on the valley floor." And he was. When he had stopped and spent that time looking down instead of joining me on the ledge, he had caught a glimpse of something which didn't look right. After thinking about it a minute, he suspected he was looking at the ground, so he took the chance and went on down, and found that the end of the rope was dangling just a few feet off the valley floor, so he safely slid off the end and was home free.

"You guys come on down, we're done with this," he called up. The Colorados came down one at a time, and when they were done, I clipped my harness back into the rope and took my turn. Once I was safely down, I pulled one side of the rope down, making the other side go up until it cleared the tree above and came cascading down around me. I coiled it as we all laughed the relieved, adrenaline-drenched laugh of those who had thought they might die but had instead survived.

It was a short walk out to the parking lot where we had left our car, which had food and water. As we chowed down, I kept thinking back to the dangling wedge on the friction slab, and to the rotted-out tree I had almost trusted with my life. I had nearly died. Twice.

Again, I couldn't believe my "luck."

6

The Outlaw Years

I loved rock climbing, but I was living and working in San Jose, California, and the drive to Yosemite was too long to make on a regular weekend basis. Then my kids were born, and I said goodbye to the climbing life. My life improved beyond anything I could have imagined due to the joy my children brought. I loved being a dad more than anything I had ever experienced. That said, sometimes the call of the wild still surged in my veins. I still needed the adrenaline rush. Fortunately, I had met some guys who introduced me to the life of wild hog poaching. I had been reading about it in newspapers and magazines for a few years, and I knew right off the bat that I'd love to try it. But since it was an outlaw subculture, the odds of meeting someone who would let me into their group were slim to none. And Slim had left town, as the saying goes.

But "luck" was with me, and about the time I phased climbing out of my life, I met up with a guy I'll call David. He had a hard time finding partners to go poaching with him because it was brutally strenuous, not to mention illegal and dangerous. A lot of guys said they wanted to hunt with him, but after the actual experience, most said, "Thank you, now don't ever invite me again." I was so exhausted the first few times I tried it that I was tempted to say the same thing. Fortunately, I always waited a few days before calling him to opt out of future adventures, and by the time David wanted to go poaching again, I had recovered sufficiently so that I was glad I had kept my mouth shut. Eventually, I got into good hog poaching shape and joined him in laughing at the flatlanders who couldn't take it.

The way it works is that the poachers go off into the night with a pack of dogs. They and their dogs can be dropped off into hog country at night by a driver with an SUV, but it also helps to know someone who lives on the edge of wild pig territory. One dog, called the strike dog, hunts loose, but the others (the "catch dogs") are held on leashes. The strike dog has to have a good nose as it tracks left and right, up and down, trying to find where hogs have been recently. The poachers walk through the hills until the strike dog finds a pig and begins barking at it. At that point, the hunters/poachers let their catch dogs off the leashes. The dogs run toward the sound of barking until they get to the pig, then they lock their teeth onto various parts of its anatomy. The hunters are not far behind, having run all the way since letting the catch dogs go, following the sound of the fight. The first poacher grabs the hog's rear legs (the pig has plenty on its mind, with four or five strong dogs biting it) and pulls the legs back and up into much the same position as if he were handling a wheelbarrow. The second hunter comes around and sticks the knife into its heart. Those are the basics, but there are endless variations. The poachers carry magnum handguns because sometimes the boar is killing the dogs before they can get there, and they have to shoot in order to save their dogs. That's a last resort, because gun shots at night can cause farmers and landowners to pick up the phone and call game wardens, and that's never a good thing for poachers. Once the kill is made, the animal is field dressed, then it is cut in half so it's easier to carry back. Each hunter can carry half the pig, draped over his shoulder. A really big pig gets quartered.

The foothills around San Jose have a massive wild hog population. Hog country extends from there all the way over to the ocean, and southward all the way to Salinas. Pigs are so prolific that the population doubles every six years despite all the hunting. Farmers hate them because they destroy crops. The Silicon Valley crowd hates them because they come down out of the hills at night and destroy golf courses and front yards in the housing tracts. With all that said, it's still illegal to hunt them at night and in the county parks, even though they kill deer fawns and other native species.

Landowners want the pigs out, want them gone, but they don't want hunters coming in either, because careless hunters can be a danger to their cattle. On top of that, it is also illegal to kill them with knives. Why? No reason, really. It just sounds cruel. I mean, we can't have these Neanderthals going out and hunting with knives. No way, this is California! Bow-hunting is legal, despite the fact that many animals are wounded by arrows and crawl off into the bushes to die painfully several days later. But hunting with knives, and killing them right there on the spot, with the pigs dying quickly, minimizing the pain? For what it's worth, hunting pigs with dogs and knives is completely legal from Texas to Florida, all along the southern states, just not in California.

So, we, the civic-minded, would go out at night into the areas where it was illegal for us to even hike (because the parks close at dusk, and private property is always illegal to outsiders), and kill these nuisances called wild pigs. We had fun doing it and always had meat in our freezers. There's nothing quite like going off into the darkness with dogs that lived for the hunt, going after animals which could easily weigh three hundred pounds, have three-inch tusks, and love to fight.

Most of the hunts were cut and dried. We'd go out and walk the hills; the dogs would find a pig, we'd run to it and make an easy kill. It was still a thrill because it's cool to be living in nature's circle of life, but no big deal beyond that. But every now and then, things got really interesting.

****

David lived across the road from a county park which had a rich population of hogs, as well as mountain lions, coyotes, skunks, and rattlesnakes. It was wild country. He called me one afternoon and said he had seen a group of hogs bed down less than a hundred yards from his kitchen window, across the road. He wanted me to bring my dog Tanner over so we could have some fun as soon as the sun went down. I loaded the dog box into my truck, and Tanner jumped into it, turned around and lay down, facing back toward me in expectation. He knew what this meant. He lived for the hunt. I closed the tailgate and we were on our way. David had called two more guys to come over with their dogs and join the party.

We all gathered in his driveway and "saddled up." This meant we donned our shoulder holsters, loaded our revolvers, and in my case, I strapped Tanner into his vest of thick leather. The vest saved his life many times over the years, preventing the boars from killing him with their tusks.

On this particular night, as we headed out, we all put our dogs on their leashes, then walked down David's driveway in the dark, crossing the main paved road at a full run to avoid any chance of being seen in the headlights of cars which might come unexpectedly around the nearby bend of the road. Once across and into the hills, David let his strike dog, Sadie, go. We didn't have long to wait before Sadie began barking furiously. We let the other dogs go, looped the leashes over our shoulders and began running to the sound of the fight, dogs versus hogs. I was older than the others and got there more slowly. When I came up behind them, David yelled at me, "Run to the right." I had no idea what he was talking about, but clearly, they had this fight under control, so I just did as he said and ran to the right. I quickly understood that we had a second fight going. Not all the dogs were on one pig. I got to the edge of the brush and saw a tunnel right at knee level, going steeply up through the thick brush. These hogs are so tough that they typically push their way through the thick brush, creating an endless maze of tunnels where no predator will follow…no predators except us.

I crouched down and shined my flashlight up the tunnel. At first, I couldn't tell what I was seeing because, as I quickly realized, a huge boar was blocking it up at the top. All I could see at the moment was fur, but I couldn't tell what was happening. As I watched, trying to figure this out, the boar moved, and Tanner came into the beam of light. He was fighting a gigantic boar all by himself. I watched for a minute more, trying to decide what to do. The boar was at least three times the size of Tanner, so if it got loose from him, it might come running straight down this tunnel. There would be no place for me to dodge, and I'd get trampled and maybe killed by this enormous boar with three-inch tusks. As I watched the fight going on through this hole, I decided Tanner wasn't going to let go anytime soon, so I gathered my courage and launched myself upward, crawling on my belly as fast as I could. "Luck" was with me and I made it all the way to the top safely. As I got to my feet, I could see it was even bigger than I had thought, and there was no one here but Tanner and me. There was no way I was even going to try to kill this one with a knife. I hauled out my big Ruger .41 magnum, cocked it, and stuck the barrel down almost touching the fur above its spine, and pulled the trigger. It spat flame in a huge roar, and the boar went down. To my horror, it got right back up again. In all the hunting I had done, I'd never heard of a boar which could withstand a 210-grain bullet shattering its spine.

Now, it's a rule of poaching that you never shoot twice. When someone in a farmhouse hears one shot, they may stop and listen, but they can't tell where it came from. But if you shoot twice, they can pinpoint which direction it came from, call the game warden or sheriff and point them in our direction. But with a boar this big, and only one dog on it, I had no choice. If I didn't get it down fast, it might kill my dog...or me. I cocked the hammer a second time, took care to get the gun barrel right over the spine, and pulled the trigger again. *Bang!* It went down again...and got back up again. This was bad. This boar was evidently one of the living dead, a zombie hog. I weighed my options, really not wanting to shoot a third time, but as I thought it over, I again came to the conclusion that I had no choice.

Just about that time another dog arrived, and behind him came David, then a third dog, which immediately joined the fight. All this transpired in just seconds, but it seemed like a long time. With three dogs and David, there might be a way to avoid shooting a third time. As we both stood with revolvers drawn, weighing our options, the big boar finally collapsed. The dogs continued to pull at it, and David put his gun away, grabbed his knife, and killed the pig for good. We had a lot of work ahead of us, getting this boar back to David's garage, as well as the first one the other guys had killed without incident. No dogs were injured, and our freezers would be full. When we dragged the boar across the road and up the driveway to David's garage, we weighed it on David's butcher's scale. It weighed two hundred seventy-five pounds, the biggest I ever saw in the hills above San Jose.

******

One of the more interesting nights of that phase of my life started out like any other average night. We had moved through the forest at night, like usual, when the strike dog began barking right in front of us. I let Tanner go as David and Tim released their dogs as well, and I took the time to loop the dog leash around my shoulder. As I moved forward with my flashlight on, something warned me this was not business as usual. The sound of the dogs on the pig wasn't quite right. I hesitated before committing to run into this, a situation where warning bells were ringing in my mind. As I stood there, I noticed something glowing in the reflected light of my flashlight.

Curious, I turned the beam away from the sound of the fight, to my right, and there, less than four feet from me, stood a trophy boar with at least three-inch tusks. It had no dogs on it at all. It was just standing there watching all the commotion. Instantly, I threw myself backward with all my strength, swearing as loud as my voice would go. David hadn't seen the boar and was running forward to get to the one pig he knew about. Now we collided as I threw myself backward into him. He couldn't figure out what was wrong with me. He'd never seen me backing away from a hog fight like this.

"Go on, grab a leg," he yelled, referring to the pig the dogs had already caught. There were so many words crowding my mind at the moment that I couldn't get any of them to come out. I couldn't settle on any one sequence of them. I wanted to yell, "Look out, there's a huge boar standing right there, and it could kill us. Get back!" But nothing came out for a long two seconds. Finally, as I pointed my flashlight beam onto the boar, I was able to shout, "There are two of them!" David turned his light in that direction, and there was that huge boar, glaring at us. We both went through the same thought process: it's a big boar…it can hurt us…we can't shoot because it's night and someone might hear us…no, we have to get to that first hog fight, but we can't get there without going by this big boy, so…we have no choice…we have to shoot. Both of us grabbed for the magnums in our shoulder holsters, brought the guns out, and…the boar simply turned invisible.

For many years after that night we relived those few seconds. The boar turned so incredibly fast that we never saw it move. It evidently just decided this commotion was disturbing its harmony, so it turned, with literally blinding speed, and departed the scene without us seeing even a flicker. It was just gone. We were both stunned by its disappearance, but didn't really have time to dwell on it, what with the initial hog fight still going on down in the creek in front of us. We re-holstered our guns and moved quickly down, holding our flashlights out to assess the situation. Two dogs were fighting a medium-sized pig in this creek, meaning the rest of the dogs were fighting yet another pig nearby. This hog was fighting for its life, dragging the two dogs farther down the creek as the fight progressed. The other guy with us, Tim, hadn't yet grabbed a rear leg, but the sow (female) was small enough that I figured I could handle her myself. So I moved in, flashlight in one hand and knife in the other.

I was never quite sure what happened, but somehow, I found myself suddenly on my back, sliding downhill with this pig on top of me. I managed to half turn onto my right side but couldn't get up with the pig weighing me down. I didn't know until later that it was a sow, so all I had on my mind was the big boar we had just seen, and somehow it was on top of me and I was sliding down this creek. I had my knife in my right hand, but it was under me as I slid. With my left hand I was pushing the pig's head away from me, so it couldn't bite me or get me with its tusks. It may have been small for a pig, maybe one hundred twenty pounds, but convert that image to "angry Rottweiler with small razor-sharp tusks, fighting for its life" and you have an accurate picture of my situation.

At this point, I was thinking, "Okay, pig, you let me go and I'll let you go." We slid downhill like that for about ten long seconds, with me trying desperately to keep those teeth and tusks away from my face. I finally hit something on the hillside which brought my slide to a stop, enabling me to roll over and shove the pig on downhill. I could hear Tim and David following it down there, trying to get into position so they could grab a rear leg as I got to my feet, emotionally out of the fight and just glad to be alive. The pig and the two dogs disappeared into a grove of laurel trees, and David followed them in. He came out just seconds later, wiping the blood off his knife. I went around the small grove, looking for the other hog fight I knew had to be going on, since a number of our dogs were still unaccounted for. I followed the sound of a pig squealing and got to them immediately. They had a small pig caught. We already had one to carry out over many miles, so we were unanimous about letting this one go. We each grabbed a couple of dogs, leashed them up, and pulled them off the small pig, which ran away as fast as it could run. We'd hunt him again someday when he grew up.

****

During those days, while hunting in the Santa Cruz mountains, a rugged wilderness, we walked onto three different marijuana farms. Pot farmers guard their crops with heavy firepower and booby traps, to avoid being ripped off by bandits who want the money-making crop without having to do the work. The first time it happened, we were hunting in the daytime and were trying to find our dog pack which had disappeared over the edge of the mountain. They had run into another canyon so fast that we really didn't know which way they had gone. We looked for them for two hours, worrying that they might be getting killed by a big boar, without us there to bail them out with our revolvers.

As we ran through the jungle-like heavy forest, we came to a dirt road. It led in the way we wanted to go anyway, so we followed it along. At the end of the road, there was a dome tent, with music playing inside it. This was really strange, in the middle of nowhere...a tent, with someone inside, evidently. David called out to whoever was in the tent, "Hey, have you heard a pack of dogs run by here?" No one replied. I had an uneasy feeling about this. David yelled, "Hey, I'm talking to you," and he kicked the side of the tent. I quickly moved away from him, thinking that if I were camped out here I'd have a gun inside the tent, and I might be tempted to shoot some redneck who came out of nowhere yelling at me and kicking my tent. Fortunately, no bullets came flying out toward us. David waited another few seconds as the music continued to play inside the tent. Then he said, "The hell with you," and he stalked away. Tim and I followed him...right into an area where at least fifty marijuana seedlings had been planted, freshly watered by an elaborate system of hoses leading back to a mountain spring.

I suddenly understood why someone was living in a tent in the middle of nowhere. I expected bullets to begin flying at any moment, but thankfully, we made it to the far side of the plants and disappeared into the thick growth beyond. David had no idea what had just happened. It never occurred to him to wonder why anyone would go to all the trouble of setting up a small farm in the middle of nowhere. He was older than Tim and me, and marijuana farming was an alien concept to him. Once the danger was explained, we took great pains to go back a different way. We crawled through a quarter-mile of hog tunnels in the thick brush rather than going back through the pot farm.

****

One night, I got separated from the other guys as we ran to a hog fight. We were hunting in an area of steep mountains above San Jose. When we heard the dogs begin fighting a pig, we were on a high ridge. The ten million lights of San Jose were way below me down on my left, while there was a deep, dark canyon on my right. The hog fight was in the canyon on the right, so I began leaping down into the darkness toward it. The other guys ran in a different direction, for some reason I couldn't understand. They were running away from where I could hear the noise. I was certain they were all going the wrong way, so I kept bounding down the mountainside, my flashlight showing me the way. When I got far down into the canyon, there were no sounds of a hog fight, and I knew I'd come the wrong way. There was nothing to do but go back as high as I could and look for the other guys. There were five of us hunting together that night, so it should have been easy for me to find them. As I topped out on the ridge, I got quite a shock. Someone had moved San Jose. I knew exactly which direction I was going, but San Jose, with all its lights, was in the exact opposite direction it should have been.

I stood there for several minutes to get my bearings and figure out what had happened. Obviously, I had gotten turned around in the dark. I walked the ridge back toward where we had been when I had heard the dogs begin barking, but couldn't hear any action going on, nor see any sign of my partners' flashlights. I searched for more than an hour, to no avail. Finally, there was nothing left to do but head back by myself. It was a vast wild area, and my buddies could be anywhere. Even if it had been daylight, I probably couldn't have found them. I was several miles from David's house, and it was going to take me a good while to get to our rendezvous point.

I had a bright moon to light the way, as long as I wasn't in a forested part of the park. I worked my way down the mountainside to where a dirt road made the going much easier. This was the main road the park rangers used as they did their jobs. It was wide enough for two cars to pass. After I had been walking for about an hour, I got a major shock. From just three feet away, a streak of something furry exploded from the grass to my right and crossed the road to my left, coming right in front of me. It moved fast, beyond anything I could imagine. Not only that, even though it was only as tall as my knees, it was incredibly long. My eyes told me that when its head was just reaching the side of the road to my left, its tail was just clearing the edge of the road on my right. In an instant, several things went through my mind. First, nothing on this continent is that long and so low to the ground. Second, what in the world could move that fast? Third, my eyes simply couldn't be telling me the truth. So, what had I seen? What just happened here?

Eliminating all the other possibilities, I finally realized I had surprised a mountain lion as it was concentrating intently on something in the grass. I had been walking quietly along, and it didn't see or hear me until I was right next to it. It was startled and ran for cover. Its apparently incredible length was due to its long tail, making the animal appear longer than it really was. I was glad it had run away, because my revolver was in its shoulder holster with the flap snapped shut, and my hunting jacket was buttoned over it. If the cougar had wanted to tangle, I'd have been dead before I could have gotten to my gun. I chalked it up to one more of the interesting things which are seen only by those who go out into the dark while the rest of humanity stays indoors watching television.

Still on an adrenaline high, I resumed my hike back to David's house. Arriving there, I took off my hunting gear and stowed it in my truck and kicked back, waiting for them to return. I was surprised to see there was a heavy coating of frost on my truck. It hadn't felt cold to me at all as I walked. They came traipsing in about two hours later, two of them burdened with half a hog each, thrown over their shoulders. We had a great time swapping our stories and hoisting cold brews.

****

I remember one night in a local county park, we had killed a good-sized pig. It was Tim's first hunt with us. Before we could even field dress it, we were challenged by a pack of coyotes who came to the sound of the fight, expecting to get to share in a kill made by one of their buddies. Imagine their surprise to find three humans standing over the pig, with fierce hunting dogs on leashes. They tried to intimidate us by circling around us, yip-yipping in protest. It was incredibly eerie, so much so that each of us had his revolver out, our backs to each other, facing outward, not knowing what to expect. After a few minutes, the coyotes realized they weren't going to win this one, so they gave up and left.

****

We were all practical jokers, constantly looking for a way to put something over on the others. One moonlit night, five of us were hunting together. We stood in a circle with my dog, Tanner, in the middle, on a hillside overlooking a large patch of thick brush where hogs love to hang out. We had two strike dogs down in the brush trying to stir up some action, when suddenly, we heard the sound of a rattlesnake angrily rattling its warning. I thought, "Oh, this is funny, as if they're going to fool me with phony rattling." I looked around at them, as they all turned and gave me the same amused look. At about the same time, we all realized it wasn't a joke at all, but really was an angry rattlesnake. Tanner had stepped on it, provoking it to rattle at us. We all exploded outward away from it as if a grenade had gone off in our midst. I jerked Tanner's dog leash as hard as I could, straight up, to get him away from the snake. By sheer "luck," none of us got bit, including Tanner. I can't remember if we got a pig that night or not.

****

We regularly poached one of the biggest cattle ranches near Hollister. The owner of the ranch didn't want hunters in there because many of them can't be trusted to shoot pigs instead of their cattle, which I totally understood. But since we only killed hogs which were caught by our dogs, there was never any confusion on our part or our dogs' as to the difference between cows and pigs. We understood the rancher's position, but being outlaws, we did our thing, regardless. The elder statesman of our poaching group, Rob (not his real name), lived on an adjacent ranch which was too small to have many pigs. However, the really big ranch next to his had zillions, it seemed. Occasionally, we went over in the middle of the night and harvested them. More often, we went at daybreak on Sunday mornings. We had found out the ranch hands who worked the big ranch went to church on Sunday, so we'd cross over at first light. We would drive our trucks to the end of a dirt road, let the dogs out of their boxes, hook them up on leashes, then walk down to a creek which served as the property line. We would cross that and hike up the other side. We kept our dogs on the leashes at this point because Rob knew the area well. We didn't hunt the rolling hills where the cattle were regularly grazed. Instead, there was a long, deep canyon beyond the rolling hills, where the cattle didn't go. The mouth of the canyon was maybe a mile from where we crossed the creek. Once into the canyon, we would let the strike dogs go, and we never came home empty-handed. Every pig we killed weighed in at roughly three hundred pounds, bigger than even the zombie boar I had killed in the hills above San Jose.

One Sunday in January, we had a weekend when none of us were free. One guy wanted to stay home and watch the NFL playoffs (city boy), others had family obligations, and so on. That being the case, none of us were eyewitnesses to what happened. Rob got up early as always, fed the livestock on his small ranch and began doing his other chores. Suddenly there was a flurry of shooting from just about the place where we'd have been if we were poaching that morning.

The more he thought about it, the more curious he got. Finally, he couldn't stand it anymore.

He drove up to the end of the road, got out, and walked the route. There's an understanding among the ranchers, that if your cows disappear, you're allowed to cross onto the next ranch to see if maybe they have somehow wandered over there. It happens. The only stipulation in this situation was that the searcher wasn't allowed to carry a gun. If you're carrying a gun, then you're hunting; if not, they assume you're just looking for some strays. So, Rob went down to the creek and up the other side, through the beautiful oak woods where the trees were adorned with Spanish moss hanging from every branch. He followed our usual trail toward the canyon, and when he got near it, he came across four dead hogs. They had been shot and dragged over to lay directly on the path we used each Sunday morning. The warning was clear. The ranch hands who worked on that big ranch had figured out what we were doing and set up an ambush. If we had done our usual, we'd have found ourselves looking down the barrels of several high-powered rifles. Their intent probably wasn't to shoot us, but rather to warn us off. Knowing myself at that stage of my life, though, and how I usually faced trouble (I always went headfirst into it regardless of the odds), I'd have gone for my gun and they'd have shot me down.

Once again, I couldn't believe my "luck."

This period of my life lasted about ten years, only ending when I realized I had a serious back injury.

7

From Caterpillar to Butterfly

At age thirty-seven, as I stood in line at McDonald's, I noticed a significant burning sensation in my left buttock. I knew something was wrong but had never heard of this symptom before. It turned out to be a classic symptom. As the months went on, it got worse and began to extend down my leg. Finally, I realized this wasn't going to just get well, so I went to a doctor. I was diagnosed with sciatica caused by a pinched nerve. The sciatic nerve runs from the back down into the leg.

I had spent thirteen years in construction, which was probably where this injury had actually begun. After getting out of the building trade, I worked in a water treatment plant, the main career of my life. As a lower level plant operator, part of my job was to drive a bobtail dump truck. Thinking I was young and bulletproof, I would jump out of the truck and land on my left leg each time I got out. After months of this, my spine had been slammed down onto the nerve where it leaves the spine and goes through the hip bone and down into the leg. Even though it could have been a simple fix with surgery, no one explained that to me at the time. Having heard all the horror stories of back operations gone wrong, I banked on the fact that I was tough enough to get through the rest of my life just on guts alone. It was a serious mistake.

Once I knew the nature of the injury, I avoided doing things which made it worse and just hoped for the best. This put an end to my hog poaching. The days of being bulletproof and indestructible were gone. Instead, for all practical purposes, I was a cripple. I had to reevaluate who and what I was. It was a time of agonizing reappraisal. I was deeply depressed. At the age of thirty-seven, I felt as if my life was over. Fortunately, I was still able to work at the water treatment facility, since most of my job consisted of computer work by then, and I could do it while sitting at a desk. The rest of the job was just walking around the plant, monitoring the process, and pushing buttons.

Seven years went by like that, toughing it out and getting by, until I made my first trip to Ireland, at age forty-four. That was a turning point for me. I loved that country so much that I wanted to go back over there as often as I could. This meant I needed to really take care of myself, so I began the process of finding a surgeon to fix my back injury. I got one who was approved by Worker's Compensation, and he did the bare minimum, which helped briefly. However, after a few months, I was right back where I had started.

I was able to make my trips to Ireland with minor difficulty from my now partly disabled leg. I didn't have to do any heavy lifting, and I could still walk up and down the hills as long as I went slowly, so I put further surgery on the back burner.

By this time of my life, I had become a hardcore atheist. My mind was focused on what I could see around me. I saw a bad world of birth defects, abused children, war, starvation, and disease. I reasoned that a loving God would never allow all this, so there could not possibly be a God who ruled the universe. I was so hardcore in my atheism that I took pleasure in debating Christians wherever I found them. I remembered a lot of the Bible from my early days, and they usually didn't know it well at all. I could tie them up in knots comparing some scriptures with others. I loved ridiculing Christians.

Having gone through a divorce some years earlier, I now had joint custody of my two kids. I joined a single parent discussion group at a local YMCA and began going on monthly outings with the group. One February, we visited Natural Bridges State Park in Santa Cruz, where the Monarch butterflies stop on their way to Canada.

The docent who led our tour explained that the Monarch life cycle begins on a mountain in Mexico. The caterpillars go into their chrysalis on the mountain. Ten days later they emerge as fully formed butterflies. Those beautiful wings didn't exist ten days earlier. That generation of Monarchs heads north for about seven hundred miles. Then they mate, lay eggs, and die. The next generation hatches, and the caterpillars grow, shedding their skin between three and five times (depending on whose research you accept). After the final time molting, they form their chrysalis. The new butterflies come out ten days after that, and *that* generation heads further north. It takes three generations to get to Canada. Every time a new monarch comes out of its chrysalis, it knows exactly which direction to go. It never gets mixed up and heads south or east or west. All this really blew my mind, because the butterfly brain is probably smaller than the head of a pin, yet it never gets mixed up. Monarch butterflies seem to be smarter than some people I know. The third generation arrives in Canada, mates, lays eggs, and dies. That new generation, which was born in Canada, begins a non-stop flight south, going all the way without dying or laying eggs. It's a two-thousand-mile journey back to that mountain in Mexico (which they have never seen)—the same mountain every time—just an eight-mile by eight-mile area where they mate, lay eggs, and die before winter sets in. In the springtime, the cycle begins all over again. They only weigh one-fifth of an ounce, and their wingspan is less than four inches. They are one of the most fragile beings on the planet, but they do this incredible migration every year. They know exactly where to go and how to get there.

Scientists tried an experiment at one point. They picked the generation which makes the two-thousand-mile journey to the south, taking some of the Monarch chrysalides to the east coast of the U.S. When the butterflies hatched, they flew directly south like all generations before them. "Somehow" they realized their mistake and turned, flying west until they were on the ancient migration route over the American midwest, then turned south and went directly to that same Mexican mountain where their ancestors had started. Later, I saw a PBS television show about it, and the narrator kept saying, "Scientists can't explain any of this."

All of this really rocked my world. I kept thinking about it and finally came to the conclusion that there had to be a Creator of some kind. I still didn't believe in the God of the Christian Bible, but obviously, Monarchs, with their sophisticated engineering, didn't happen by a random roll of any cosmic dice. I was looking at the fingerprint of an intelligent Creator. So, what now?

I still couldn't get around all the suffering in the world. So I surmised that a god of some kind must have created all this beauty, then sat back and let things happen randomly after creation. After creating all these symbiotic life forms, he seemed to have just let it all fall apart. I later found out that the theory of God somehow winding a watch, then letting it go on ticking without any further involvement is called Deism. I thought I was the first person to figure all this out, but eventually learned that it had all been thought of before. Many of America's founding fathers were Deists: Thomas Jefferson, Ben Franklin, Thomas Paine, and many more.

By this time, my daughter was 13 years old and was a born-again Christian. I wanted to be with her as much as possible, given the joint custody with her mother, so I offered to go to church with her on Sundays as a way of our having good quality time together. We found a church which had a preacher she liked, and they played great upbeat music, so we began attending regularly. I figured it was just a social thing, never giving any thought to any of the church stuff being based on reality. After two years, things began to take shape in my mind. I was listening to the preacher speak one Sunday when—with no warning—I began to cry. It was so powerful that it was almost like projectile tears. It had nothing to do with the preacher trying to milk my emotions. He wasn't preaching about anything sad. In fact, I can't even remember what he was saying. I just began to cry uncontrollably, unrelated to anything going on up in the front of the church. I had to really struggle to get myself together before my daughter noticed, because I had no way of explaining this to her. We went out to lunch after the service was over, and as she talked, I kept thinking, "What happened to me back there?" I had no idea. About a month later, it happened again, exactly the same as the first time, with no warning. As it came on me this second time, I had a realization: this was a very real God showing me something. I had heard of this before, when I was a teenager, folks talking about how "the Holy Spirit was dealing with them." This had to be what they were talking about. I wasn't under any kind of stress; I wasn't sad or upset about anything. I had learned to live with my disability and the pain in my leg. I just couldn't stop this fountain of tears. But now it had happened twice, and I knew something supernatural was working inside me. I still didn't understand it, but I couldn't deny that something beyond me was happening.

Having been a vocal, outspoken atheist, I had been ready for someone who knew me from my workplace to come up in the church lobby and ask me what I was doing there. The answer I had ready was: "I am here so I can have quality time with my daughter. So back off, buddy!" I didn't give it much thought until a few weeks after my latest "surprise crying" episode when my daughter went on vacation with her mom for a couple of weeks. I woke up on that Sunday morning thinking, "What if the pastor says something funny in his sermon (which happened a lot), and I'm not there to hear it?" It was football season, but suddenly it was more important that I hear the pastor than watch the NFL. I still didn't want to be confronted in the church lobby by those I had pontificated to about the nonexistence of God, so I drove there and parked where I could see the church entrance. When the service started and the greeters at the door went in to begin worshipping, I got out of my car and sneaked in, sitting in the back row. At the end, when the pastor began the final prayer, I got up and left in a hurry to keep anyone from talking to me. As I drove home, I thought, "You know, I'm in serious trouble. I'm beginning to believe all this is true."

A few weeks later, some life-altering events happened to me—things that for various reasons I cannot detail here. I hadn't seen them coming, and they rocked my world like nothing ever had before. I was pushed to the edge, giving serious thought to suicide. My mind went back to what had happened to me in church, when the tears had begun flowing "for no reason." Now I saw that I needed God desperately, and I knelt down at home and began seeking God with my whole heart. I cried out to Him, told Him that I finally understood that He was real, and I begged Him to come into my heart and forgive my sins. Nothing happened. After a few minutes, I got up and sat down on the couch that I had been using as an altar. I was in shock. Now that this outlaw was done running from Him and fighting Him, it seemed He didn't want me. I had waited too long, gone too far. Now I had nothing to look forward to except an eternity in hell, which I now believed was as real as God.

This was the pattern I lived for the next three days. I'd kneel down and beg for forgiveness, telling Him I was sorry, that I now realized He was real, and I wanted to spend the rest of my life serving Him. Nothing. I'd get up and go run some errands and come home, get on my knees and seek forgiveness again. Nothing. I'd pray for ten or fifteen minutes, then give up in despair. A few hours later, I'd do the same thing again, because...well, there was no other option. It was either God forgave me, or...an end to everything. The three days seemed like an eternity to me. I remember that when I had served God as an eleven-year-old, how unmistakable it is when God comes into a heart and forgives. And this wasn't it. I felt no release from my fear, no forgiveness, no forgiving Presence of love and joy in my heart. Finally, on the third day, I made up my mind. There was nothing left to live for. If God didn't show up that day, I was going to commit suicide. The things which had brought me to this point were things I couldn't live with, and I was finished if God didn't want me back. However, praise God, that afternoon as I prayed, He came back in and filled my heart with Himself. Much to my shock, He accepted me back. I crossed from death to life, as the Bible says in John 5:24. For most people, it doesn't take three days of desperate prayer for God to accept the prayer of salvation, but I was an extreme case. I had lived a life of ridiculing the Bible and persecuting Christians, and God really put me through some serious spiritual refining.

I got up off my knees, turned around, and sat down on the couch to figure out my next moves. I thought back to what I had known about living for God in my teen years, and it involved three things. One, spending time each day with God, one-on-one for worship and for spiritual feeding. Okay, I could do that. Two, reading out of the Bible each day, partly in worship, but also for learning and hearing from God. Okay, I'd get a modern version of the Bible and get to work. I could do that. Third, a Christian is faithful in going to church regularly for fellowship, learning, and to encourage others. Okay, I could *not* do that. My shift had just rotated, and I was now working Sundays. As I sat thinking about it, I remembered there were mid-week study groups at the church I had been attending with my daughter. I began looking through the pile of papers on my dining room table and found an old church bulletin with the main phone number on it. I called the church and found out a new group was starting that very night, taught by the pastor I had come to respect. I couldn't believe my "luck."

My whole life took on new meaning as I studied the Bible and explored truth for the first time since I was a teenager, twenty-eight years earlier. I spent a lot of time each day seeking greater depth in my relationship with God. The supernatural transformation of the inner man had begun. As the months went on and I grew in my knowledge of Him, it was odd looking back at my old life and comparing it to the new one. My anger was gone, and with it went my propensity for knee-jerk violence. I was glad for that, but wondered how I'd face my old need for adrenaline. All I could figure was that my need for speed must be displeasing to God, so I would just try to explore this reborn person whom God was cleansing. I wasn't happy thinking that my need for excitement would never be lived out again, but it seemed there was no choice. Either we served God or welcomed death. We would either spend eternity with God, being rewarded, or with Satan, sharing his punishment.

Physically, though, I was going downhill. One year after my coming back to Jesus, at age forty-eight, I realized that I was close to needing a wheelchair. I began going through the process of finding a better doctor than I had the first time around and getting the surgery approved by Worker's Compensation. It took about eight months, but it was worth it.

Initially, the new doctor examined me and refused to operate. He told me, "If you had come to me a few years ago I could have given you a full recovery, but now the damage is done. I have a six-week waiting list of patients I can actually help. I'm not going to do surgery when I can see it won't do any good."

I was blown away. God was living in my heart and mind, but this was still heavy news. As we sat looking at each other for a long moment, the surgeon had a new thought. "There's one more test I can run. It involves injecting dye into your spine and seeing where the dye can reach and where it can't because of obstructions. The difference between this new test and all the ones I've already run is like looking at the shadows on the face of Half Dome in the morning versus the evening." He set the test up, and it was worse than the surgery ended up being, but from the results of it, he decided I had a seventy percent chance of getting significantly better. We moved forward and scheduled the operation.

Although I would never be 100% again, at least I could walk after this operation, and the majority of the pain was gone. No one looking at me could tell I was disabled. I was grateful I could walk at all, and it was icing on the cake that I could still hike the local mountains as long as I went slowly. I'd never backpack Yosemite or go hunting in the Bighorn mountains of Wyoming again, but I wasn't going to complain at this point.

My kids had moved in full time with their mother during the week I came back to Jesus. The timing was purely coincidental. They were tired of having to change houses every few days with the split custody, and I didn't blame them. I gave some serious thought to my priorities at this point in my life. I was renting a three-bedroom home so my kids could each have their own room, and now that they were gone, I saw this as a major waste of money. I owned a van which was set up for camping. It had thick carpet, curtains for the windows, and plenty of room for me to stretch out and sleep comfortably. I worked in the water treatment plant three days or nights per week, twelve-hour shifts. On those days/nights that I worked, I could finish my twelve-hour shift, make some dinner in the plant kitchen, then walk out to the parking lot, crawl into my van, and go to sleep. On my days off, I could park it pretty much anywhere and sleep. The only hard part when I worked nights was finding shade during the day (I began this lifestyle in the heat of September) so I could sleep. When the weather turned cold, I was all set. I had all my camping gear from the old hunting days, so staying warm was never a problem. At one point, a friend asked me what my daughter thought of my new lifestyle. I hadn't really given any thought to that, but now I wondered. So, the next time I saw her, I asked if she thought what I was doing was weird. She thought seriously for a moment, then said, "Not compared to everything else you do, Dad." I had to laugh. "Yep," I thought, "right on target."

My pastor saw how I was living and took pity on me. He offered to let me sleep in the church lobby on my nights off, as a kind of unpaid night watchman. That was helpful.

This phase of my life lasted four and a half months. When the van kept breaking down, I got an apartment in one of the worst neighborhoods in San Jose. I didn't realize how crime-ridden the area was. I was just looking to live as cheaply as possible. One day, as I sat reading the newspaper, I saw an article about the San Jose police declaring war on gangs in a four-block area. I felt bad for the folks living there until I looked at the map in the article and realized I lived in that four-block area. It was business as usual for my unusual life.

Looking back now, I can see that God was repurposing me, repurposing the way I was wired—seeking the thrills, craving more adventures, pushing through fears—to work for Him in new fields where those traits would be essential. He had been "preparing a great fish" for a future He had planned even before I was born. All those times I expected to die but didn't, weren't "luck." God had been there, keeping me alive, because He had work for me to do.

8

The Preparation Continues

When I prayed about getting married again, I asked God to give me a lady who would enjoy traveling as much as I did. Then I met Donna, who had come to the Lord about two years after me. We had both come to Jesus in the same church. The first time we had lunch together I regaled her with stories of my latest Ireland adventure as she listened patiently. When I finally shut up and gave her a chance to talk, she told me of a trip to Italy which she and her mother had already booked, and that they were planning a trip to Scotland after that. We were a match made in Heaven. We were married less than a year later and honeymooned in Ireland.

Shortly after we got married, I opened my email one day to see a letter from my pastor asking if I would be interested in going to Israel with him. It was three and a half years since I had come back to Jesus, and I wanted to see the Holy Land. However, at that time, there was serious unrest in Israel, an intifada, and there were videos of the violence on the news every night. Tourism had dropped off to virtually nothing, and the tour companies were offering fantastic deals, especially to pastors. My pastor was being offered a great price, and he could bring a friend along at the same price per person. But even after seeing the low cost, I knew I had to say no, because we didn't have the money for both Donna and me to go. I hit reply and typed out a note saying, "Thanks, I'd love to, but we can't afford it."

Before I hit send, though, I went in to where Donna was making dinner and told her of the offer. She said, "Well, you can go if you want to, but I'm too scared to do it." I ran back to the computer, deleted everything I had previously typed, wrote, "I'm in. Let's do it!" and hit send. I began counting the days. This was my first time going to a foreign country other than Ireland, and I had no idea what to expect. In addition, there was an extension at the end of the trip, to Egypt. That was another exotic place I'd always wanted to see but never thought I'd get the chance. It was only one full day there, and two nights, but hey, I was going to get to see the pyramids.

As the weeks went by and I got the packing checklist from the tour company, Donna was a bundle of nerves. She kept telling me, "I have a bad feeling about this," hoping I'd back out of the trip. I just nodded and smiled. Actually, for an adrenaline junkie like me, this was perfection. I hoped I'd see some newsworthy events taking place and get pictures of them. As things worked out, one week before we left for the Holy Land, a peace agreement was signed. There was a prominent picture on the front page of our local newspaper with the Prime Minister of Israel shaking hands with the head of the current intifada. Now there would be peace for our tour.

We flew to Frankfurt, Germany, changed planes, and went through all the extra security checks to get from one terminal to another, then on to the boarding gate for Israel. There were many orthodox Jews on this flight, which surprised me at first, but made sense after I thought about it. During the time we spent waiting to board our plane, some of them donned prayer shawls and went into a corner together to pray. I had never seen this kind of thing before. As they prayed, they swayed, dipping their torsos forward, then upright again, time after time. I found out later it's part of their culture to pray in this manner. They are deliberately imitating the flickering of a candle as they pray. Seeing this, my Israel experience began right then, ironically, in Germany.

The flight from there to Israel was a short one. We landed at Tel Aviv-Ben Gurion Airport, went through Customs, and were met by our guide. We were bussed to the hotel where we'd spend the night. As the bus drove us along a modern freeway, my first cultural experience was that, for the first time in my life, I was in a country where I couldn't read the billboards. They were all in Hebrew. It was like being a small child again and needing the grownups to read for me. Except for that, I could have been in any city in America with all the buildings and regular traffic I was used to seeing.

This was more jet lag than I had ever experienced before, but nothing like I'd see in the years to come. The bed was a welcome sight when we checked in to the hotel. The next morning, I went out the sliding glass door of our hotel room, which was on the ground floor, and walked a hundred yards to the Mediterranean Sea. I called my wife on my specially purchased international phone and held it out for her to hear the small waves lapping at the shore, and said, "Guess what you're hearing? That's the Mediterranean!" For a history buff like me, this was as good as it gets, beginning my day on the shore of one of the most important bodies of water in history. I could just imagine Roman or Phoenician ships anchored out there.

The whole trip was like that, one incredible historic place after another, and the vast majority of them were biblical places like Jerusalem, Bethlehem, the Dead Sea, the Red Sea, and Ein Gedi. We even got to spend two nights in a kibbutz on the shore of the Sea of Galilee.

The foods were exotic to a guy like me who had never eaten schnitzel or falafels. As we ate breakfast in the mornings, I made friends with some young Palestinian men who brought us coffee, and I learned how to say "Thank you" and "You're welcome" in Arabic.

The Bible came alive for me in a way I never imagined. After coming back to Jesus, I certainly believed the Bible stories were true, but now that I stood on the Mount of Olives and looked down to the Temple Mount where Jesus had taught daily and where Solomon's Temple had stood a thousand years even before that, it all took on a reality which changed my life. After getting back home, I couldn't get enough of the Old Testament. Now I could picture Isaiah and Jeremiah down there speaking the Word of the Lord to the rebellious children of Israel. At night, I could look down from my hotel balcony on the modern streets of Jerusalem and imagine how fearful it must have been to see an Assyrian army camped down there...or the Babylonians...or the Romans, besieging the Holy City. It had all happened right there.

Everywhere we went, we saw people carrying guns. Some wore sidearms, some carried M-16 assault rifles, and there was the occasional Uzi. It was a sober reminder that the Israelis face powerful enemies on all sides, and they never know when they'll have to fight for their lives against a terrorist attack.

I felt safe, for the most part, but I knew violence could erupt at any moment. One day, our tour bus stopped at a Palestinian-owned gift shop (this was not unusual—the shop owners are friendly to Christian tourists; everyone has to make a living) so we could buy mementos of our trip. It was a good-sized store, and our group filtered out among the aisles. I filled my shopping basket, then went to the cash register which was in the center of the store, next to a stairway to the second level. The store owner rang up my purchases himself and was all smiles as we made conversation. He was pulling in a nice haul from our busload. "More power to him," I thought. He was a big guy, an older man, about six-foot-three inches tall and in his mid-fifties. Just as I was thinking about how big he was, the door opened, and three young Palestinian men walked in, all in their mid-twenties. The store owner had his back to the door and didn't see them at first, but warning bells began ringing in my head. The three young guys were carbon copies of each other, about one hundred forty pounds and five-foot five-inches tall. They weren't threatening because of their size. It was something else. The three spread out, leaving about twenty feet between each of them as if they expected shooting to break out and didn't want to all get hit with the burst of an automatic weapon.

One of them positioned himself at the foot of the stairs, eyeing the store owner from the side. That young man was smirking arrogantly, waiting for the owner to notice him. Given the amount of danger they radiated, I looked them over again, more closely this time to see if I needed to look for cover immediately. I was a bit comforted that they wore skin-tight white T-shirts and blue jeans, almost like uniforms. To my guarded relief, there was no room in their clothing for concealed handguns or suicide bomb vests. I relaxed a bit until the store owner noticed something out of the corner of his eye and turned to look. His mood changed instantly, and deep fear came over his face. With my purchase halfway rung up, he left the cash register without a thought and went over to the smirking young man. I couldn't understand their Arabic, but the owner was clearly pleading with the young guy about something. I looked around for our tour guide, who was our mother hen for this week, our protector and our barometer of danger. I saw he was in deep conversation with a group from our bus, explaining something historical or biblical to his captivated audience. I didn't feel like I had the authority to tell him to get everyone outside, so I just stayed where I was and hoped for the best. The conversation at the bottom of the stairway lasted almost five tense minutes, with the store owner pleading with the arrogant young man about something.

From what I had read of life in this part of the Middle East, I thought I understood what I was seeing happen here. The store owner was big enough to thrash all three of these small guys in an instant, but it wasn't these three who struck fear into him. It was the organization which stood behind them that scared him. If they couldn't come to terms on whatever these guys were expecting, his store would be firebombed, or his family would be hurt. Or his car would blow up some morning when he tried to start it. And if he somehow was able to get these three locked up by the police, all their hundreds of buddies on the outside would take their revenge. There was no way for him to win this, hence the instant fear when he saw them. This wasn't the first time these guys had met each other.

Still smirking, the young Palestinian by the stairs turned, collected his comrades, and went back out the door. The owner came back and finished adding up my purchase, but his mood had been ruined, and his warm smile was a thing of the past.

I loved every minute of the trip for the spiritual aspect and my new understanding of the Bible, despite the possibility of danger. I heard sporadic gunfire while I was there, which I later found out is not unusual for that part of the world. To me, it was all part of the adventure. Being there instilled a deep hunger in me to see the rest of the world. My first exposure to an area where languages other than English were spoken stirred up a strong wanderlust in me, but I never thought I'd have a chance to live it out.

All too soon, my first trip to Israel was over, and we were driven to the border of Egypt. The Israeli bus was not allowed to cross, so we had to collect our luggage and walk across the border. We went through no less than six passport checks. As I waited in one line at the border, I looked up to a nearby hill and saw an Egyptian flag flying just a few yards from the Israeli flag. That was apparently the exact border, and I thought it would make a poignant picture. As I brought my camera up and focused it, I got a sharp reprimand from one of the guards, his AK-47 slung over his shoulder. He took an aggressive step toward me, shaking his head at me. I got the idea and lowered my camera. If I pushed this, I'd get my camera confiscated.

These guys were scared to death of the tiny country of Israel, as if those radical Jews might actually invade Egypt and take the country over. The city of Cairo alone contains more people than the entire country of Israel, yet the Egyptians are remarkably fearful of being invaded.

We began the six-hour bus ride to Cairo, crossing the seemingly endless desert of the Sinai Peninsula, as our guide entertained us with the history of the area. We crossed under the Suez Canal via the Ahmed Hamdi Tunnel, named for Ahmed Hamdi, an Egyptian engineer and general killed in action during the 1973 Yom Kippur War against Israel. As we reached Cairo, the cameras came out and the frenzy began, taking pictures of the pyramids we could see in the far distance. None of us stopped to think we'd be standing right there beside them tomorrow and get even better pictures. We checked into our hotel and had a nice evening after a buffet-style dinner before turning in for the night.

The next morning, we boarded our bus after breakfast and went to see the pyramids. Once again, I was overwhelmed at all the history right there in front of me. The biggest one, called the Great Pyramid, is estimated to have been finished around 2560 B.C. It has a tunnel inside it, leading to a burial chamber for the pharaoh who commissioned the pyramid, Cheops. I found out that for only twenty dollars American, I could enter it and climb to the top of the tunnel. It was a small price to pay for a great adventure.

I got my first taste of being shaken down for money by foreign authorities. I had just exited the Great Pyramid and was walking around taking pictures of it from every angle. Walking up close to it, I stooped down to get a shot of it from the bottom of one of the corners, when three Egyptian soldiers with rifles came running up to me.

"Get off the pyramid." shouted their leader.

"I wasn't on the pyramid," I snapped back at him.

"Give me your camera," he ordered. Reluctantly, I handed it over to him. If he confiscated it, there wasn't much I could do about it. He had the authority to arrest me if he so desired. I hoped I'd get my camera back, since it had all my Israel pictures on it, and I didn't expect to ever get back there again.

He turned it on and said, "Stand over there at the corner of the pyramid." Now I saw where this was going. I walked over there and stood, and he took my picture, then handed the camera back to me.

I had wanted to get a picture of some Egyptian soldiers but knew better than to get caught doing so without their permission. Now I had a golden opportunity, and I knew they wouldn't refuse me because they were seeing dollar signs.

I asked them to pose at the corner of the pyramid, and they obliged, with their rifles slung over their shoulders. When I was done, the spokesman held his hand out and said, "Now you help us." I had gotten money from the hotel ATM last night, and my heart sank as I remembered I only had big bills. Mentally, I did some math. Fifty dollars of Egyptian money was only eight dollars American. I could live with it. I got out my wallet and handed him a fifty. He nodded, and they walked away. I had gotten off lightly. It could have been much worse. As I walked away, I noticed another soldier out of the corner of my eye, this one mounted on a camel. I would have loved to get his picture, but I knew it would be more money out of my pocket, so I decided against it. He saw me and called over, "Hey. Hey you. Come here. Hey. Hey." He was far enough away so I knew I could get away with pretending not to hear him. Our tour group only had a short time left there, so I went back and stood next to our guide at the bus and stayed there until it was time to leave for the trip back to the hotel.

Egypt was a much rougher place than Israel, which was a much rougher place than Ireland, which was a much rougher place than Canada. God was preparing a great fish…and the next phase of my preparation was soon to come.

9

First Taste of Missions

Later in the same year of my Israel/Egypt trip, I accompanied a pastor friend of mine on a trip to India, my first mission trip. It was a tame trip compared to how they can go at times, but it was still a step up the ladder from anything I had seen so far. My adventure began before I even left home. I made an appointment with a doctor who specialized in travel medicine. Never having needed this kind of doctor before, I made the appointment for two weeks before my departure date. I filled out all the forms explaining where I was headed and the date of my departure. He went over the paperwork, then set it aside and began telling me where the dangers lay for me.

"In the area where you are going, Japanese encephalitis is rampant. It's fatal, and there is no cure. It's imperative that you get vaccinated for it before you leave. Now, the shots are administered in a series over four weeks…wait, when are you leaving?" He looked at his notes and said, "Two weeks. Ah. Well, never mind about those. Make sure you use lots of mosquito repellent."

As I sat there wide-eyed, digesting this and planning on how many gallons of repellent I could fit into my suitcase, he went on. "The next important thing for you to know is that dogs are everywhere in India, and we average one patient in here every month who has contracted rabies from a dog bite while they were there. The shots are one hundred percent effective. They are administered one week apart over a span of four weeks...wait, when are you leaving? Ah...never mind." I made a mental note to wear my high-top boots.

The one thing he was able to provide (which ended up saving my life) was a prescription for a powerful antibiotic to be taken in case of food poisoning. I will be forever grateful for it.

There was no physical danger to us in India (although beatings of the local Christians are not rare, as we learned), but the culture shock was still huge. For one thing, it was about as far as you can fly in the world before you're actually heading back toward home, having circumnavigated the globe. The journey is an extremely long one. But worse was the smell of the air as we walked out of the terminal in Delhi. Our noses were hit with a stench, a mixture of diesel fumes, urine, and other unidentifiable odors. A few months after getting home, I saw a sitcom where one of the characters said, "That's the worst thing I've ever smelled, and I'm from India." I knew exactly what he was talking about. The diesel fumes were so bad, the street lights had halos around them, much like you'd expect to see on a foggy night in London. To make it even more bizarre, as we exited the terminal, there were hoards of taxi drivers behind barricades calling to us, trying to get us to hire them. It was surreal. We were relieved to finally see our Indian hosts there waiting for us beyond the taxi drivers.

We had met a third traveler on the plane, also a pastor from San Jose. We were all there to see about supporting a certain Christian ministry which reaches the very poor. The car ride to the small hotel where we would be staying was a wild, nightmarish adventure of dodging between lanes, slamming on the brakes, then pedal-to-the-metal fanatical acceleration, horn honking the whole time. We were playing chicken with the cars in other lanes who wanted to compete for the opening in a third lane which our driver saw at the same time the other driver did. Numerous times, I gave up any hope of getting to the hotel without serious disaster. During my time in Cairo earlier that year, one of our group had told me I owed it to myself to go up to the roof of our hotel and watch the circus of traffic negotiating the roundabout down below. Several of us went up and watched for hours as the cars aimed at each other, sometimes bumping, sometimes dodging, to claim a brief space in the lanes, some of them bluffing, some not bluffing but homicidal, it seemed. I now longed for those safe days of Cairo traffic. To say I was praying intensely would be an understatement. Several times, I thought we were just one coat of paint away from a collision. There were lines on the pavement, but no one paid any attention to them. And to take it into the comical, even our driver, the leader of the Christian organization we had come to visit, Pastor Joseph, honked incessantly at all the red lights, even when there were five cars in front of him and there was no place for them to go. When we asked him why he was honking, he shrugged and said, "I don't know. Everyone does it." And yes, they did. As the week went on, I noticed most of the red stop lights had the word "Relax" printed on them in big letters, in English. Thinking back now, it's amazing I ever got a chance to see those red lights with the English word on them, given that he only stopped at red lights if other cars were coming. If not, we just barreled through them. They were quite a nuisance, after all, and we were busy people.

I was surprised to see Pastor Joseph was driving a brand-new car. It had less than fifty miles on it. Given his maniacal driving, I wondered how it was that he had a brand-new car. He told us it was a loaner from a supporter of the ministry and would be given back to him after we left to go back to America next week. During our wild ride, he hit several speed bumps at full throttle without a second thought. I didn't see how the car could hold together, being abused like that. As we were soon to see, it couldn't.

We arrived at our small hotel. It was late at night, and a uniformed man opened the gate for us and closed it behind us. Driving up to the front door, we retrieved our luggage from the trunk and went into the lobby to check in, with Pastor Joseph translating. The elevator taking us up to our floor was tiny, adding to my impression that this place had been built decades ago when the British still ruled India. Looking out the window of our room, I saw there were many people wandering the streets below. I understood why there was a gate which had to be opened from the inside. There are entire generations of Indians who are born on the streets, live their whole lives there, and die there, never having lived inside a building.

The next day, we had the afternoon free and spent some time walking the streets. Every so often, there was a large tent pitched on the sidewalk, and we could see cots in there. Whole families were living in them. I did some exploring every morning, and I came to understand a lot more about the street people, just by observation. They live in those tents (if they have them at all; many don't), sleeping however they can. Some have cots to get them off the pavement, some don't. Sometimes there were a number of tents pitched next to each other on the sidewalk, forming a community. In the mornings, I saw people arriving and hauling propane tanks around, which puzzled me at first. As the darkness turned into daylight, these propane haulers set up stoves and began cooking bread. The homeless people emerged from their tents and lined up to pay the small amounts they could afford for the bread which is their breakfast. There are also many small kiosks up and down every street selling teabags and hot water. The homeless, or anyone else, can buy a morning cup of tea, inexpensively. It is a whole economy based on providing the homeless with their basic needs, with the providers making their living in this way. Among the many services I saw offered were open-air barber shops, tailors sitting at their sewing machines, and bicycle repair shops doing business on the sidewalk. Many of these tent people have steady jobs. When breakfast is over, and they've had their tea, I saw some disappear into their tents and emerge later in the uniform of hotel staff. They can make enough to subsist, just not enough to live in houses like we are used to here in the U.S.

One thing I had never seen before was the many beggars. It's heartbreaking, but you can't really give to them without being mobbed by hordes of their friends who are watching from a distance. If you give them every penny you have, there will still be more coming at a run after seeing you hand out money. The only way around it is not to give to any of them, ever. It was a hard policy to make myself obey, but there was honestly no way around it. I forced myself to think about why we were there: to see about supporting this Christian organization which worked in the slums helping people like the ones I saw right outside my car window each day as we drove through the city.

Right before we arrived in Delhi, a series of bombs went off, killing more than sixty people and scaring everyone—especially the government—so all Christian meetings were put on hold. In India, the government can do that. Christians have to get their church services approved each week, and now they had all been canceled. Shortly after our arrival, the restriction was lifted, but for our first full day there, we had no plans, so Pastor Joseph tried to show us around the city of Delhi. I say "tried" because the government had also shut down a lot of the tourist attractions, such as the India Gate and the Red Fort, which we visited but couldn't go inside. We had to content ourselves with taking pictures of each other in front of it.

Pastor Joseph took us on a walk through the downtown area. On one block, there was a sidewalk bazaar with a number of people trying to make a living however they could. One guy had a sewing machine and a sign which read, "Zippers fixed while you wait." I found it interesting that the sign was in English as well as Hindi. There was also a wide variety of clothing for sale, hanging on racks for our perusal. Another vendor had many pairs of shoes, all used and worn.

During my Israel/Egypt trip, I had developed a love of coins from around the world of any historical or cultural interest. Now we came across a man sitting with his legs folded under him, offering coins of all types for sale, some of them ancient. They were displayed on cloths laid out for that purpose. I noticed the man had several fingers missing, which reminded me of my grandfather, who had been a cabinet maker until he was in his eighties. He was too old to be doing that kind of work and would frequently cut off the end of a finger, sometimes just a bit, sometimes more than a bit. I assumed this coin seller had been a similar kind of tradesman and must have lost too many fingers, having to step down to a new way of life, selling coins on a sidewalk. Maybe I could give him some business, and we'd both benefit. I looked at many he had to offer and asked Pastor Joseph to give me the history of all the ones he recognized. I began bargaining with the seller, with Joseph as the interpreter. The seller asked one price and I haggled with him in the time-honored tradition of all traders, worldwide. I wanted older coins, of which he had many. I gave him an offer on one set I picked out. He said, through Joseph, that his children would starve, and icebergs would clog the Ganges River, causing major loss of life, if he let me have the coins so cheaply. I came back with a counter-offer, saying I had had a terrible childhood, but if I could only get these coins at a lower price it would bring immense healing to my whole family, including cousins I had never met but hoped to someday. He couldn't possibly sell the ones I wanted for that price but could let me have newer and less intriguing ones for the money I was offering. We went back and forth for a while, then he stopped arguing and gathered up the coins I had picked. I was convinced my superior bargaining skill had won the day. I gave him the money we had settled on. He put my coins into a bag, handed them to me, and we walked away.

As we strolled away down the sidewalk, my pastor friend said in a hushed tone, "Do you think that guy might have had leprosy?" A sick feeling kicked me in the stomach as I thought of the seller's missing fingers and the fact that he had sat with his feet curled under him the whole time, so I never saw them.

It all came together in my mind, and I said, "Well, *now* I do. Why didn't you say anything before I touched the coins?" He made no reply but looked as ill as I now felt. I dug into my backpack and got out the hand sanitizer and drenched my hands until they dripped, rubbing them together.

My pastor friend said, "Don't worry, it's not contagious. People used to think it was, but now we know better." I hurried up to where Pastor Joseph was walking ahead of us and asked him about it.

He said, "Oh yes, very contagious." His fellow pastors agreed when I questioned them later, "yes, very contagious." When I got home, I did a web search and found out that, although contagious, it is not spread through casual contact. I breathed a sigh of relief.

There is a significant postscript to the story. When I arrived back home in California, I spread newspapers over the floor so I could see the coins without having to actually touch them again. As I began bragging to my wife about how I had outfoxed this guy with my superior American know-how, I poured the bag of coins out onto the newspaper. That was the first time I realized that after all my haggling with the guy, as I had turned to smirk to my buddies about the deal I had made, he had done a switch of the bags and given me a different one, with much less valuable, commonplace coins. This guy, with not much in the way of fingers, had done a sleight of hand which would have done justice to an accomplished magician. Wherever you are, buddy, let me just pay tribute to you and your skill. Well done, sir. I got outsmarted, and I still smile when I think about it.

When the bombing crisis had abated somewhat, we were allowed to go to the slum church which was run by Pastor Joseph's organization. On Sunday it was a church, but Monday through Friday, it was a school with more than three hundred students. Joseph told us the brand-new car he had been driving was now "broken," but refused to explain how it had happened. He had arranged to come pick us up in a taxi. The driver was a turbaned Sikh, looking professional in his fine clothes. He held the door open for us, closed it behind us, and we were on our way. He was a much better driver than Joseph, thank God. The traffic was still bad, but at least this man knew how to navigate it safely.

When we turned off the main paved street, our driver finally realized where we were asking him to take us, and an argument broke out between him and Joseph. Things got tense and it became obvious that he was refusing to take his nice taxi into this slum. After a few minutes, the driver won the argument and we got out and had to walk the rest of the way. That was quite a wake-up call. Our driver looked as tough as anyone I've ever seen. With his turban and his Sikh beard, he looked like he'd be the first one hired if you were putting together a crew of pirates. If he didn't think it was safe in this slum, it made my adrenaline pump to think about lambs like us going in there.

Pastor Joseph told us this slum held more than a million people, divided between Hindus and Muslims. Now that he had started a school, there were Christians here as well. There was no pavement at all because the government did not wish to waste money on a slum. There was no running water, and the electricity was sporadic. Even now in December, the weather was hot, and during the summer, the temperature regularly got up to 118 degrees Fahrenheit. I mention this because in this slum the dwellings were all built together, touching each other on all sides except the front. This meant there were only doors and no windows, thus no way to get any cross ventilation. The back wall of each unit was also the back wall of another unit on the other side of the building. Each dwelling was like an oven.

The church/school was three stories high, but it could only be entered by bending down and going into the only doorway, at ground level. One of the reasons we were here in Delhi was because the Indian government was shutting the school down due to inadequate fire exits. Make that *no* fire exits other than the front door on the ground level, which wasn't even normal height. There had been a fire in another school not long ago, with terrible loss of life, and the government was now cracking down on all schools. The government didn't offer any kind of schools in these slums but would shut down any which didn't have adequate fire safety, no matter who was running them. Our church back home was considering donating money for a new school. Pastor Joseph's organization already had purchased the land for the new school, but had no money to build, so we were looking at what they were doing, to see if we were interested in helping them.

After taking a few seconds to look in on the service which was in progress at ground level, we went upstairs, stopping at the second level for a moment to see the different church service going on there. Both of these meetings and the one on the third floor were going on at the same time and were part of the same overall church. Each level had their services tailored to the particular languages of the parishioners. When we reached the top level, we were escorted to the front, where chairs had been placed for us as the honored guests. The room itself was sixty-five feet long by twelve feet wide (slightly larger than a boxcar), and the services below were in identically-sized sanctuaries. The worshipers sat on the floor, on thin carpets. The men sat on one side of the sanctuary, the women on the other. As we walked in, they were on their feet, singing their hearts out, clapping, and many of them were jumping up and down in their enthusiasm. Drums and electric guitars played with no concern about what effect it might have on the neighborhood around them. As I later found out, the neighbors on the other side of the wall were Hindus on the south and Muslims on the north.

I had met Pastor Joseph in California as he was going around to local Bay Area churches, drumming up support for his organization. I told him I'd go, but before agreeing to it, I made it abundantly clear that I was not a preacher, nor did I ever want to be one. I added, "I will come see what you are doing in northern India, but don't expect me to get up in front of a congregation." Now that we were there, Pastor Joseph instructed the three of us to each take an hour to preach a sermon. What? "No!" I retorted, "I'm not a preacher. Ever. I told you that from the beginning." He tried to calm me down by assuring me I need only take half an hour to preach. I was upset, feeling I had been conned. I told him no how, no way would I preach. Actually, public speaking is one of my greatest fears. I had climbed mountains in Yosemite and killed wild boars with a knife in moonlight, but speaking in front of a crowd? Are you kidding me? That is scary beyond measure. Finally, I had an idea. I had been learning to play the Irish penny whistle, and there was one in my backpack at the moment. I told him I'd play "Amazing Grace," the only Christian tune I could play at this point in my life. He agreed on that, and when the time came, I stood up, gathered my courage, and tortured them with my rendition of the hymn on my Irish whistle. They suffered through it with dignity, for which I was grateful. For the rest of our time in India, I dutifully got up and played the whistle whenever I was called upon to greet the people and was thankfully spared the duty of preaching to people who were expecting quality encouragement from America.

One interesting aspect of every church service we attended was that these poor people would walk for miles to come see us, or ride bicycles if they were wealthy enough to have one. Many of them were homeless, but as soon as the singing stopped, we could hear cell phones ringing throughout the congregation. They might not have a roof over their heads or food to eat, but they all have cell phones. I finally realized that cell phones were necessary to them for survival, all the more so if they had no home.

When Pastor Joseph's service was over, we moved outside in front of the church. The Christians fellowshipped with each other while I took a short walk around the neighborhood. Mothers were bathing their babies in basins out in front of their hovels. I wondered where they got the water. I found the answer to my question when a government water tanker came driving down an alley which passed for a street in this slum. It pulled up to a water tank I hadn't noticed before and began filling it. I, the American water treatment plant operator, began to wonder just how clean the inside of the tanker was, where he had procured the water, and if it was treated to kill bacteria. Before he had been there long, pumping into the tank, a line of people formed who had been waiting and watching for him to arrive.

As I walked back to where the Christians were visiting, a man passed me with a single-shot 12-gauge shotgun slung over his shoulder. I was startled and looked around to see if anyone was alarmed by it. No one seemed to notice. I heard later that security guards are allowed to carry them for work, so it was likely just a man coming home from his job.

Being pre-diabetic, I refrained as much as possible from eating the rice and bread which formed the staple of Indian dining. We ate breakfast and dinner each day in the restaurant on the ground floor of the small hotel where we were staying. Although they offered a variety of dishes in the evenings, the mornings were monotonous to someone trying to stay away from sweet rolls and croissants. I had been warned by my travel doctor to not eat anything unless it had been cooked. One of the most common ways of getting sick in a developing country is to put seasonings on food. Peppers and other kinds of condiments are grown in the fields where animals graze freely, such as the sacred cows which are seen pretty much everywhere in India. The peppers are harvested, ground up, and put into packages, without ever having been cooked to disinfect them. In my water treatment classes, I had been taught that heating food or water to one hundred and eighty degrees Fahrenheit will kill the germs which cause the many different types of food and water-borne diseases. But in most developing countries, India included, cooking the pepper wasn't considered necessary. So my travel doctor, who had lived in India for many years, told me to never eat anything such as salad or fruit, and to never use seasonings on anything I ate. I lived by that rule for the first few days, but I got bored with the breakfast routine.

I decided to eat the beautiful papaya set on the table each morning, the one which had been peeled, washed in hotel water, and then set on our table. That was at 7:30 a.m. At 2:30 the following morning, I woke up feeling a bit nauseated. By 4 a.m. I was lunging for the bathroom, barely making it before the projectile vomiting began. I knew I was in trouble. I got the food poisoning meds out of my backpack, took the first pill and lay back down on my bed, hoping for the best. Fortunately, the time between vomiting bouts was long enough so the medicine was able to get into my system, but the vomiting didn't stop until around 10 a.m. By that time, I had made numerous trips to the toilet. My travel partner had given up on sleep and gone down to the lobby with a book to get away from the terrible noises I was making. When it came time for breakfast and being picked up by Pastor Joseph, he had to leave me there and carry on with the other San Jose pastor. I lay there all day, weak and helpless. Even as weak as I was, I still got bored. Eventually, I gathered up my strength and made the pilgrimage across the room to my backpack to get my iPod. Back on the bed, I picked my favorite playlist, all songs from the Christian rock band, Kutless. As bad as I felt, it was still wonderful to hear them singing in my earbuds. They were a marvelous comfort to me. It was like having family with me there in this hostile land. There was a television in the room, but I was too sick to care.

In the afternoon, I actually got hungry, although food still didn't sound good. I called room service and ordered a hamburger and french fries, with no condiments, no tomatoes, and no lettuce. I was learning. I knew everything in that lunch order had to be cooked. When the food arrived, I opened the container and my stomach revolted, so I lay back down. But lying down, I was hungry again. I got back up, walked across the room to the food (I didn't want to smell it any more than I had to, so I exiled it as far away as I could), opened the container, and thought of taking a bite of the hamburger. Again, my stomach said, "No." So I picked up a french fry and stuck it in my mouth. My stomach said, "Well, maybe." I walked back to the bed and lay down. The potato sat well on my stomach. After a few minutes, the hunger returned, so I made the journey back to the food and got one more french fry, then back to bed. Sure enough, it felt good in my stomach, and I was hungry again soon. I thought, "Well, I'll just eat the whole order at once and be done with it." My stomach said, "No, you won't." So I ate the whole order of french fries, one fry at a time over the course of the whole afternoon. Lesson learned. God was continuing to prepare a fish: being hungry is less bad than eating tainted food.

The next day, we had planned a trip to see the Taj Mahal, and there was no way I was going to miss it. Thankfully, I was no longer nauseated, but I was still feeble for the next few days. I probably would have died without the antibiotic. The local pastors tried to talk us out of making the four-hour drive to see the Taj, telling us it was overrated, and most people ended up disappointed. We had given them our complete attention for this whole week, and now we wanted to see something which we'd probably never again have the chance to see. We got up at 4:45 a.m. and ordered breakfast. All they had at that hour was toast and butter, but that might have been all I could handle anyway.

We went down to the lobby at 5:45, and our driver came walking in five minutes later. He had slept in the car, so he wouldn't be late. We got into his Mercedes, and five minutes later we stopped at a gas station. He fueled up the vehicle in the darkened station as a guard walked back and forth with a single-shot 12-gauge shotgun slung over his shoulder. I whispered to our driver, asking if he thought the guard would get mad if I took his picture. He whispered back, "Yes." I left my camera in its belt pouch. I have a lifelong rule which has served me well: never make a guy mad when he's carrying a shotgun.

It was still pitch dark as we began the journey. We passed many trucks driving with no lights, so our driver had to be careful. At one point when we were on a stretch of divided highway, I saw a car coming toward us on our side of the road. I was alarmed and wondered what was going on. Our driver wasn't fazed, but just continued along the road as we met the car and went on by. I guess what Pastor Joseph had said about not knowing why there were lines painted on the pavement also applied to which side of the road people drive on...whichever side they want to, evidently. Traffic laws were mere casual suggestions. As the trip went on, we met many more vehicles on our side of the road. We even saw some on the correct side.

When the sun came up, we began to see trucks headed to work, with crews of laborers stacked on top, getting a lift to wherever they would spend their day working. Many of the trucks also had guys on bicycles holding onto the rear corners of the truck so they wouldn't have to pedal. These guys must have been further up the food chain, since they could afford bikes. My guess was that at the end of the work day they could pedal back home or wherever they wanted to go. I wondered how the others got home.

At one point, we passed a small caravan of wagons being pulled by camels. Our driver heard us exclaim about it, so he pulled over and waited while I ran back to get pictures. The drivers appeared to think we were strange to want their pictures, but they adapted quickly, holding out their hands for money. I gave them ten rupees each, about twenty-five cents in American money. They were happy, and we were soon back on our way again.

Every so often, we'd hit an area where our noses were assaulted by a sickening stench, like Delhi but even worse. Within a few minutes, we'd drive by a village of many hundreds of people living with no running water, nor any kind of sewage treatment. It broke my heart to think that generations were born there, lived and died there, never knowing any other life. I guessed many of the men from those slum towns were on the tops of the trucks we passed, on their way to work to earn whatever meager wages they could, to provide for their families.

We stopped at roughly the halfway point at a tourist-oriented restaurant for breakfast. They had actual western-style toilets, as opposed to the squat toilets which were more commonly seen in typical Indian establishments. We all ordered french toast, and I was able to eat. My appetite was beginning to come back in a small way.

At one point, we drove through an area where there was a large crowd of people all around us. There was a beautiful Hindu temple there, and our driver explained that the people were there attending a significant festival. We stopped the car and got out for pictures. I was still weak and shaky from the previous day's adventure in Indian dining. I didn't feel up to carrying on a conversation, but an American stepped out of the crowd and asked us where we were from. He lit up when we said, "The Bay Area." He was from Santa Barbara, a few hundred miles to the south of our home. It's such a small world, indeed. The following day, we were telling Pastor Joseph about seeing the festival, and my buddy asked him what would have happened if we had tried to witness to them about Jesus. His reply: "You would have been killed immediately."

We finally reached Sikandra, near Agra, where the Taj Mahal was located. We stopped unexpectedly and picked up an articulate young man who was to be our guide for the day. This hadn't been talked about or agreed upon, but he ended up being indispensable, because he was amazingly informed about the history of the area and was an excellent teacher.

Our next stop was Akbar's Tomb—again not what we expected—but an excellent bonus on the day's tour. It was built between 1605–1613 for one of the Mughal emperors. It is situated on one hundred nineteen beautifully maintained acres which are home to baboons and antelope.

After enjoying a tour of the tomb and getting some good pictures, we were back on the road to Agra. Our driver dropped us off in the parking lot of the Taj Mahal, and our young guide got out with us. We gave him the money for the entrance fee, and he went to get the tickets for us. We walked between some tall trees along a path where swarming monkeys tried to get our attention, hoping we'd give them something to eat. Many people did. Meeting our young guide at the main entrance, we all had to go through metal detectors, and anything resembling a tool or knife had to be checked into lockers provided for this purpose.

The Taj was breathtaking beyond our expectations. The craftsmanship of inlaid marble was more than I thought mankind was capable of producing with just hand tools. We greatly enjoyed our guide's tour. He was an interesting young man whose father was Muslim, but his mother was Hindu. When we were surprised by this, he told us they just never talked religion, and it worked for them.

After touring the Taj Mahal, we were driven to a restaurant with safe food, and then we were given a tour of Fort Agra. It had a fascinating history dating back to the sixteenth century. Emperor Shah Jahan, the builder of the Taj Mahal, had made it his residence. Interestingly, his son deposed him, and Fort Agra actually became a prison for him—a luxurious one—but still a prison. For the rest of his life, he could look over the walls of Fort Agra and see the Taj which he had built as an exquisite burial monument for his wife.

The drive home was uneventful. We arrived back at the hotel at 9 p.m. The cost for the day was twenty-six American dollars for car, driver, and guide. We tipped the driver and guide eleven dollars each, probably more than they had seen in a long time. I was glad we hadn't paid attention to the pastors who had tried to talk us out of making the trip to Agra.

The next day was our last one in India. I was still shaky from the food poisoning. Having no great agenda, we slept late and checked out of the hotel at noon. After Pastor Joseph picked us up in a van, we collected two more Indian pastors, and we drove out of Delhi. We passed historic Tughlak Fort, with monkeys swarming its walls, driving up into the hills. We were on our way to see a new church which had just been started in a town which, in English, would translate to "monkey town." Hinduism has more than thirty million gods, and this town was dedicated to a monkey god.

Getting food poisoning had caused me to feel down in the dumps, overwhelmed by Delhi with all its multitude of nauseating smells. To my great pleasure, our route took us up out of the urine- and diesel-permeated smog and into fresh air and bright sunshine. My spirits soared, and all seemed right with the world for the first time since we arrived. But then, every half-hour or so, we would once again "smell Delhi," and sure enough, within a few minutes we'd drive by a slum village where hundreds lived with no running water or sanitation. Each time my heart would break for them.

We arrived at "monkey town" and drove through it slowly on the dirt road. The residents walked back and forth in front of our car, living their lives, glancing briefly at us, then losing interest as more important matters were on their minds. I saw several small children with the distended bellies of malnutrition. That was made more infuriating by the sight of numerous wild pigs running around the village, with no one making any effort to eat them. Given my background, it seemed cruel to allow pigs to live and children to starve. One of the Indian pastors reminded me that Hindus don't eat meat, and Muslims don't eat pork. Well, that explained it, although it was still galling to see. The culture clash in my mind was huge. My first thought was that if I lived here, I'd do some serious hog poaching and never have to worry about having enough to eat. Only in later years did I come to understand how naive I was that day. If I had cooked a pig for dinner, I'd have been in serious trouble from angry mobs as soon as they smelled the cooking pork. There was just no way out of it, except to introduce these people to Jesus.

We got to the new church and took a lot of pictures. The Christians had erected a cross on top of the small building, an act of real courage in a town like this. We held a ceremony to break ground for the new work which was going to expand the church building to eventually be home to an orphanage. We prayed together over it and sang songs together. As we got ready to leave, the pastor of this new church brought out a platter of beautiful fruit. I hated to turn down their hospitality, but I had learned my lesson. I declined with a smile, hoping I wasn't being rude.

When the dedication was complete, we drove back into Delhi where Pastor Joseph and his staff treated us to one last dinner. Pizza this time. What joy, American food! I watched as Pastor Jacob interrogated our waiter when he brought bottles of water to our table. He closely examined each of the bottles, slowly opening them while listening intently as the plastic lids popped when the seal broke on each one before nodding his head in satisfaction and passing them on to us. This was good street wisdom on his part. We'd have been lost without these good men taking care of us all week long.

There were three of us on one side of the table, all Americans, and three Indian pastors on the other side. They wanted to get our thoughts on what it was like being in their country for the first time. When the question was put to me, I explained that India was a beautiful country with much to see, and it had many wonderful people I had enjoyed meeting. However, I had had a hard time adjusting to the air pollution. The Indians were flabbergasted, looking at each other in consternation. Finally, one of them spoke for all, "What air pollution? There's no pollution here." All three of us looked at each other in astonishment. Then the pastors explained that the government had passed laws within the last few years, coming down hard on manufacturers to reduce the air pollution, and what we now saw was a vast improvement over what existed before. Up until then, asthma among school children was almost epidemic, and now with the new laws, the rate of respiratory illnesses among children had dropped dramatically.

Dinner over, we were driven to the airport and escorted in to get our boarding passes. We said our goodbyes, bidding our Indian brothers farewell.

The first leg of our flight was from Delhi to Chicago and was sixteen hours in the air before touching down. I hadn't known planes could be this long in the air without refueling. After a brief layover in Chicago, it seemed like a short flight home to San Jose and safe food.

This had been a tremendous education for me, a whole new level of international adventure for me, this time for God. He was preparing a fish.

10

The Next Step

As Donna and I began our life together, we thought it would be a life of studying the Bible with each other, living our lives as witnesses in California, and that would be pretty much all there was to it. Then two years after we got married, a deep restlessness settled into my heart. It wasn't a restlessness regarding our marriage. It was something else entirely. It was a bit like a fish dreaming about having lungs. When I met Jesus, God filled a hole in my life I hadn't even realized existed, but now there seemed to be a new, smaller hole I couldn't quite define. At the age of fifty-three, I discovered an organization which smuggled Bibles into countries where they are illegal. There are at least fifty-one countries where Christians languish without access to God's Word. They are faithful to Him, but they starve for what we are privileged to enjoy on a daily basis. I didn't even have to think about it; I knew immediately that I had found my calling. I went through the application process, was approved, and began a new life of fulfillment in using the oddball personality God had given me. Before, I had been a renegade living for myself, now I would be an outlaw for God.

As part of the application process, I had to list two references who would put in a good recommendation for me. One was easy; my pastor was happy to do it. The second was a guy I had known since high school, now a pastor, and he also agreed to do it for me.

As we talked later, though, he said, "I want you to know I'm completely opposed to what you're doing." I was flabbergasted. How could anyone be against getting Bibles to our brothers and sisters in restricted countries? He said, "You're breaking the laws of those countries, and the Bible teaches us to obey those in authority over us." I asked him how he could think like that when it was obviously so crucial for our spiritual lives to spend time in God's Word every day. He stuck to his more narrow interpretation of Romans 13:1 and 1 Peter 2:13. I think we need to balance them with Acts 4:19: "Judge for yourselves whether it's right in God's sight to obey you rather than God," and Acts 5:29: "We must obey God rather than men." (NIV)

As I was to find out later, many Christians share my friend's point of view. I thought about the fact that both Peter and Paul were executed for refusing to obey the Roman authorities when ordered to stop preaching about Jesus. And I considered that when we are commanded to live lives of love (Ephesians 5:2), it means providing whatever we can to make it possible for our brothers and sisters to survive under persecution. It doesn't seem loving to leave the Christians twisting in the wind rather than providing them the basics they need for the nourishment of their souls. I feel strongly that it's actually sinful to care more about obeying tyrannical leaders than caring for their victims. It's imperative that we do whatever it takes to supply the believers with God's Word. James 4:17 (NIV) says, "If anyone, then, knows the good they ought to do and doesn't do it, it is sin for them." It would have been a sin for me to refuse to smuggle Bibles to those who can't get them legally.

When I got the phone call telling me I was approved to join the ranks of people who do this kind of work, the trip coordinator and I picked a date for my first trip. The destination would be China. The coordinator, Mary (not her real name), helped me make the plane reservations, which I paid for myself, as all travelers in this kind of ministry do. As we discussed the details of my joining this group, I seemed to recall something I had read on their website about their providing all the training which would be required. In my mind, I thought it meant they offered a class at their national office. Since I had Mary on the phone, I asked when the training session would be held. I needed to make plans to take time off work, so I could travel to the organization's headquarters. There was a pause, then Mary said in a small voice, "There's no training session." There was a much longer pause then as I wondered how in the world I was going to get training for Bible smuggling, if this were the case.

I had a nagging worry that this was just the tip of the iceberg, so I moved on to the next question I had been wanting to ask, "Upon my arrival into the area of operation, who will be meeting me at the airport?" She replied quietly, "No one." Now I was truly stunned. There was a much longer silence. Then she went on, "As a matter of fact, we'll give you instructions on how to catch a bus from the airport. It's a forty-five-minute ride to where you will be met by one of our people who live in that city. I'll give you details about where to get off the bus when the time comes." I was speechless now. What kind of fly-by-night organization was this? If they wanted me to carry Bibles across borders for them, the least they could do was pick me up at the airport, right? There was another long silence as I thought this over. Mary was quiet, giving me time to think. My mind was racing. This wasn't what I had signed up for. I had first read about Bible smuggling when I was sixteen years old, and I thought it was something I was perfectly gifted to do, even way back then, before my rebellion and my years in "the wilderness." Now here I was, having found an organization which did exactly that, and having actually been accepted to join the team.... But now this. Did I give it up and back out, because it was going to be rougher than I thought? I had ridden a motorcycle through a tornado, been shaken down by Egyptian soldiers, and been to the slums of Delhi. Was I going to let this defeat me? No!

"Okay, I'm on board," I told Mary. She set up my flights, and I was on my way. I did have one follow up question, though, before we hung up the phone. "Do you want a picture of me to show the people who'll be there when I get off the bus?"

She said it wouldn't be necessary. I asked how they'd know how to find me in a large crowd. She chuckled and said, "Oh, that'll be easy. You'll be the one looking lost." As things turned out, she was right.

As my day went on after talking with Mary, I kept wondering just how sophisticated this Bible smuggling operation could possibly be, to not even offer a lift from the airport to the apartments where the smugglers bunked between operations. I was signing on with a bunch of losers, obviously. After several hours, a light dawned on me. There could be no better weeding-out process than this. Anyone who was uncomfortable with these arrangements would also be uncomfortable with putting a suitcase full of Bibles onto a conveyor belt, then just praying and trusting God as they watched it go through an x-ray machine. Brilliant. And so, it proved to be.

Mary was wrong about one thing. It wasn't a forty-five-minute bus ride. It took an hour and fifteen minutes to get from the airport to the appointed bus stop. Thankfully, Mary had been right about not needing a picture of me, though. As I stepped off the bus, a young lady stepped up to me and asked, "Is your name Darvis?"

11

Things Get Serious

In April of 2007, I spent two weeks in China. During my time there, I made five border crossings with Bibles. On my last crossing, we started the day out with the usual briefing at the secret company office. This involved getting detailed instructions concerning where we were going, who we were meeting, and how we were getting there. We typically concluded the meeting by singing several worship songs and spent some time in prayer. It was my turn to pick the songs that day. I only picked two, "What a Friend We Have in Jesus" and "Tis So Sweet to Trust in Jesus." Then for some reason, I really wanted us to sing one more, "How Great Thou Art." It's my favorite Christian hymn, and I was surprised at myself for not thinking of it first. After singing it, we prayed, and it was time to go.

The packs of Bibles had been loaded into opaque waterproof bags (called "rice bags") for us by the local staff. We each chose a suitcase from the rack against the wall, put the heavy rice bags into the suitcases, and off we went to catch the commuter train which ran to the border.

We crossed into China easily, putting our suitcases onto the conveyor belt which carried them into the x-ray machines. As usual, God worked His miracle of having the x-ray folks talking among themselves instead of watching the screens and catching us. I had gotten used to it in the previous two weeks, and—although it's always a moment of prayer and concern—all went well, and we continued on our way without incident.

On this particular occasion, two of us were carrying Bibles, but my buddy and I were carrying empty suitcases.

Outside the Customs area, the two who were carrying Bibles hailed a taxi and left for the airport, about an hour away. I took my friend, "The Texan," with me, and we rode the escalators deep underground to the subway train. It's amazing how far underground the Chinese subway system goes. Once down there, we traveled into the heart of this gigantic Chinese city. We got off at our designated stop and climbed the stairs up to ground level. The company we were working with had rented an apartment in one of the many skyscrapers, which served as an in-country warehouse for the Bibles. There were scores of well-labeled cardboard boxes there, containing many kinds of Bibles as well as Sunday School lessons, song-books, and every kind of literature an underground church needs in order to prosper. We had been given detailed instructions about which boxes to open and how many Bibles of each type to get. We found the right boxes easily and filled our rice bags. Loading them into the suitcases, we took the elevator back down to ground level. From there, we caught our own taxi to the airport and met up with the rest of the team at a prearranged spot.

When the time was right, we went over to the ticket counter to check our luggage and get our boarding passes. This was the same team I had been working with for the whole two weeks I had been in China. We had taken turns being leader, and it was now my turn. This meant it was my job to get everyone's passport and give them to the ticket lady along with our e-ticket paperwork. The others had brought their suitcases full of Bibles, parked them next to me at the counter and walked away to wait for the next step. After giving the lady our paperwork, I picked up the suitcases and put them on her scale. She started the conveyor belt which pulled them back where she could put the destination tags on them. As she did her work, I let my mind wander back over the last two weeks. I was feeling pretty good. I had never been caught on any of the five border crossings, and really, this kind of work was easy. I made up my mind to come back to China as often as time and money would allow, taking God's Word to my brothers and sisters. I wanted to do this for the rest of my life. Yep, I am pretty much God's James Bond, no stranger to danger....

I snapped back to reality when I saw the ticket agent angrily waving at me to look behind her. When I did, my whole world changed. There was an angry airport security officer standing at a table back there, and he had my suitcase on it. He was waving his hand at me, commanding me to come back there with him. At that moment, I saw something which had escaped my attention. Between the ticket agent and the security officer, there was another x-ray machine, one that I had not anticipated at all. The officer had seen the Bibles on his monitor, and now we were about as busted as we could be. I went from being God's James Bond to being a scared little boy who just wanted to go home to mommy, but there was no place to hide. My heart was trying to thump its way out of my chest. I didn't have time for an ornate, flowery prayer. I simply began praying, "Oh Lord, oh Lord, oh Lord…" endlessly. He knew what I meant.

We had been told that if you are caught with the Bibles at the border, it's really no big deal. They confiscate them, give you a claim ticket, and you can pick them up on your way back across the border for a small fee. It's like a game, played out between border guards and smugglers. But at this moment in history, it was a different matter if you got caught with Bibles inside China. I knew they weren't going to kill us or lock us up and throw away the key, but we had all heard of the three Australians who had been caught a few months earlier. They had been interrogated for seventy-two hours by Chinese authorities who spoke English just as well as they did. They had to go through every picture on their digital cameras and name every person in every picture. They had to go through every number in their cell phones and explain who everyone was and why their number was in the phone. Once the authorities had squeezed every molecule of information from them, they were driven to the airport, where they were ordered to pull out a credit card and pay an exorbitant price to be on the next plane back home. Their passports were stamped with red ink declaring that they were not allowed back into the country. So, while I knew we weren't going to die, I also knew the next few days were not going to be fun for any of us.

There was no way out, nowhere to run. I had no choice but to go back there to him. I sent up the most heartfelt 911 prayer of my life, up to that point (is there such a thing as 911 squared?), and walked back to where he had the suitcase on a table. He thumped it with his hand, demanding "Open." I had no choice, so I unzipped the suitcase. The Bibles inside were hidden within the rice bag, which he thumped and again said, "Open." I took a deep breath and opened the second bag. This was clearly beyond my ability to fix. I could do nothing but relax into my trust of God. If He wanted me to be arrested as a witness or even just for my own refining, I was totally submitted to His will. There were the Bibles, in plain sight. It was clear what they were, black leather-bound books with Chinese writing on the cover. They were contained in a transparent bag of thick, strong plastic.

Now the cat was out of the bag. I studied the security man's face to see if I could fathom what would happen next. An expression of surprise came on his face. He stood there for several seconds, then bent forward and pressed the plastic down onto the Bibles. He ran his fingers slowly over the Chinese characters. He straightened up and seemed to be puzzled. He looked like he was trying to remember what he had been going to say. The seconds ticked by (hours, to me). He was getting more and more agitated. Finally, he motioned to me to pick up the whole plastic bag of Bibles. I didn't understand what he wanted, but I did as he showed me. He was pantomiming what he wanted me to do now. I guess his English was limited. I picked up the bag, and he glared intensely at the air beneath it. Then he stepped back, and I set it down. More time ticked by. He motioned for me to move it up and to one side. I did as ordered, and he looked closely at the empty bottom of the suitcase there, too. Then I set it back down. Now my eyes were riveted on him. Something supernatural was going on here. Chinese culture can't stand "losing face," and this security officer was losing it in a big way, more so as each moment ticked by. It finally dawned on me that God had confused his mind, and he simply couldn't remember why we were there or what we were doing. Cautious hope rose up in me, as the "Oh Lord, oh Lord" prayer continued intensely.

We both stood there for perhaps twenty more seconds, with his expression going back and forth from agitation to confusion. At length, he made an angry wave with his hand, snarled wordlessly, turned, and walked away. I was astonished but didn't waste any time zipping up the bags and putting the suitcase back onto the luggage conveyor belt. It already had its destination tag. I walked back over to the team. They had seen what was going on and had been praying intensely, too. My hands were shaking an 8.5 on the Richter scale as

I told them what had happened. We walked away praising the Lord for working a miracle right before our eyes.

As I walked toward my gate for departure, I felt God speak into my mind, "Was that enough adrenaline for you, boy? I have lots more, if that wasn't enough." God created humor, and now he was breathing His smile into my heart.

But the story didn't end there. We caught our flight, and as we landed at our destination, we kept our seats rather than fight for the aisle to get off the plane. We were in no hurry. We weren't connecting to any other flights, so we let the Chinese locals disembark first. As we sat there on the plane, music began playing on the plane's speaker, which had been silent through the whole flight. It was a beautiful piano solo. As I listened, I began to smile, thinking, "That's funny. It sounds almost like the opening notes of 'How Great Thou Art.' I must have the song on my brain because we sang it this morning." The next musical phrase sounded like the second phrase of the same song, then the third phrase came, and I realized this Communist Chinese airliner was playing my all-time favorite hymn!

I nudged the Texan on my left and said, "Am I hearing this music right?"

He said "You sure are, it's 'How Great Thou Art.'"

I turned to the British lady on my right and asked, "Do you hear this, too?"

She said, "Yes, that's the song my husband and I had played at our wedding forty years ago."

I called across the aisle to the lady from Virginia and told her to listen to the music playing on the speaker. She listened for a moment. Then her eyes went wide, and she said, "If an American airliner played this song, the ACLU would file a lawsuit, and there would be picket lines protesting it."

It was like the Lord was placing His benediction on our trip, saying, "I was here all along, keeping you safe and making sure the job got done. I know you love this song, so here it is as a gift from me."

I realized much later that God knew someday doubters would come along, saying the airport security guy who didn't arrest us must have just had a bad day, or maybe had just gotten bad news from home. But no one could ever doubt this miracle of hearing my favorite hymn played on a Communist Chinese airline.

****

Over the years, I made five trips to China doing this kind of work. The teams were always international ones with people coming from all over the world to take part.

We always had to keep our suitcases under the weight limit the airlines allowed, and sometimes it took a lot of scratching my head to make it work. It became a way of life to take three sets of clothes for a two-week trip. Every couple of days we had to do our laundry in the hotel sink. Once I knew this life was for me, I bought quick-drying travel clothes, but even so, I frequently had to put on wet clothes in the morning and let my body heat dry them out. It was just a routine part of adventure travel.

On one occasion, we were carrying so much "Precious Cargo" that there was no room for our clothing or anything else, such as a toothbrush. Fortunately, I wore a bigger than average fanny pack when I traveled internationally, so I put one set of t-shirt and underwear into it, with a toothbrush. Once we arrived at our destination, I found a place to buy deodorant and toothpaste.

These journeys to China were the beginning of my serious mission trips. After I had made a few and had a basic idea of how things worked, a pattern became apparent. When it came time to buy plane tickets, the money came in miraculously. It always looked like a coincidence. Sometimes, I'd get to work overtime because someone else called in sick. Other times, just as the deadline came, we'd get a tax refund check for that year. In addition, due to my getting paid every two weeks, there were two months out of the year when I got three paychecks instead of two. I was frequently invited to speak to my church about the most recent trip I'd been on. Because of this, there were times when people would come up to me and say they'd like to help out with expenses for the next trip. I made it a point to never ask for money in any way. I accepted what people offered, but I never even hinted that I needed help. That way, I knew God had His hand on me for the upcoming trip. The miracles began before I ever set foot on an airplane.

****

One of the more interesting things about traveling in China is that no matter where you go, you will see small elderly women wearing bring orange reflective vests and bamboo hats, sweeping the streets and sidewalks. They use homemade brooms (made from branches of trees, with the whisks being comprised of leaves). These tiny women are everywhere. They always fascinated me, so I enjoyed taking pictures of them whenever I got the chance. China must have the cleanest streets and sidewalks in the world.

In September of 2007, I was part of a team taking Bibles into central China. Our team numbered eleven travelers, with people coming from England, New Zealand, Denmark, France, Australia, and the United States.

We flew to a large city in central China and made our first delivery. The following day, we took a four-hour train ride to a smaller city which had never received Bibles from us before. As we rode the train, our team leader went into some detail about not knowing what to expect when we arrived. We had all heard stories of the jubilant reaction among Chinese Christians who may have been praying for a Bible of their own for years, maybe even decades. Our leader told us how some weep for joy, while others just clutch the Bible to their chest, hanging on for dear life as if they fear it may disappear.

When we reached our destination, we grabbed our suitcases full of Bibles and exited the train into the station. I was last in line, which enabled me to see what happened next. There were ten "westerners with heavy suitcases" in front of me as we walked in single file. There in front of us was one of those tiny Chinese sweeping ladies hard at work. I was watching her, fascinated as always. I saw her look up from her work, then frown in consternation at what she was seeing. Her eyes swept from the front of our line to the back, then again. Who were these gigantic (to her) westerners emerging from the train station? Then I saw the light of recognition come into her eyes. A beautiful smile lit up her face, and she began waving frantically, saying probably the only English word she knew, time after time, "Hello, hello, hello!" as she waved. She turned and looked behind her toward a man (who was also sweeping) about her own age whom I hadn't seen until this moment, and she began speaking rapid-fire Mandarin to him. He also frowned in confusion, then lit up just as she had done. He too began smiling and waving in joy and saying, "Hello, hello, hello!" Instantly, I understood what I was seeing. These two underground children of God had been praying for a long time to have a copy of God's Word. They had been told that when the "westerners with the heavy suitcases" arrived, they'd finally get to live their dream, to have a Bible they could call their own.

We all broke into smiles and waved joyfully back. As I waved, I thought, "Sister, you and I don't speak the same earthly language, but someday in heaven, we will talk with each other about this moment, and we will laugh again together at the memory."

We continued out of the station and met our contact, who took delivery of the Bibles. I have no doubt the sweeping lady and her friend got their Bibles later that night.

****

On my second trip to China, I was warned by my new teammates that they had been getting caught constantly as they went across the border. The authorities were really watching for us. On average, only one out of four of them were getting through with the Bibles. We weren't in danger, but it was frustrating to lose our Precious Cargo. Sure enough, later that day as we all tried a simple crossing to stock one of the safe houses, they really hammered us. They stopped me and many others right off the bat. Being "stopped" is the slang we used, meaning that we got our materials confiscated. We were all frustrated and depressed about it. We hadn't come all this way from around the world just to have our materials taken away.

The following day, we embarked on a four-day chain of deliveries which began with crossing the border then catching a plane. We started off with the same lousy average: only twenty-five percent got through. I was blessed to be one who got through, but the other three of my small team were really down in the dumps. Each of the other teams had identical numbers. There were 11 of us in the overall group, crossing the border in three groups to keep us from all being scooped up together. Only three of us got through with the materials.

On the China side of the border, those who had been stopped made a visit to one of the safe houses to replenish what had been confiscated. Then we all met at the airport to continue our long trip. We had a great time over the next few days, seeing many interesting places in China, meeting with Christians there, and making deliveries along the way. During one of the conversations on the trip, our leader, who lived in China full time, said there was another way of getting across, but it meant leaving early in the morning and going on an extremely convoluted route to avoid the crossing where the guards seemed to be expecting us. We were unanimously in favor of it, no matter how early we had to get up. We just wanted to accomplish our task, to bear some fruit for the Lord.

So, on our next border crossing, we went against the obvious. The flat where we were bunked was just a short ride to the border crossing. It had been picked for that reason, easy access. But this time, we rose early in the morning and took the train going the opposite way, away from the border. Reaching our stop, we exited the train and transferred to the underground commuter subway, which took us down to the waterfront. There, we split up into smaller groups, taking taxi cabs to the place where we caught a high-speed hydrofoil boat that took us up a river for a full hour. When we got off, we went through a backwater Customs office where a sheepish lady in uniform watched with an embarrassed smile as we cruised past her x-ray machine, refusing to stop. We caught a bus that took us the long ride back to an airport near the border. There, we got off the bus, went into the terminal at "Departures," rode the elevator up to "Arrivals," and exited as if we had just flown in. We took a shuttle bus back to the border, where we were only half a mile from where we began our day, but now we were on the inside of China.

It had been a long morning, and now it was noon. We stopped for lunch, then split into two smaller groups. Five of us were continuing on to make the delivery while the other six were going back across the border, out of China. They would make a number of quick border crossings over the next couple of days, restocking safe houses where the supply of Bibles had been recently depleted.

The five of us who remained in China wheeled our suitcases over to the bus station and bought tickets to a city which was some four hours east of us. There were warnings posted all around notifying the citizens that a Level One typhoon was blowing in. We simply trusted God to keep His hand on us. When the time came, we put our luggage into the compartments and got on board the bus. Before we left, a security officer came on board with a video camera and went down the aisle, getting everyone's face on film for any future reference the government might want. It was an eerie feeling, but this was the way the Chinese bus system worked. It was nothing new. Then we were on our way.

As we rode onward, a television monitor at the front of the bus played endless martial arts movies. The rain was pouring, and the wind was howling. The typhoon was clearly assaulting this part of China. We passed numerous eighteen-wheelers which had been knocked onto their sides. But whenever our bus would be rocked, an Unseen Hand held us firmly on the road. Finally, we got to the right bus station. The rain pelted us as we climbed down and walked around to the luggage doors of the bus. We retrieved our suitcases and stood around looking for our contact. The visibility was poor due to the heavy downpour. We began walking out to the street through ankle-deep water, and finally I spotted our contact. I had been on this run before, so had no problem recognizing her. She is known for her legendary smile. We shook hands all around, beaming in God's joy. We loaded the suitcases into the trunks of cars which had arrived for that purpose. Then we expected her to leave, but she didn't. She directed us to a street bus stop with a roof overhead, so we were out of the rain, and she insisted through hand gestures that we wait there. Because of the language barrier, we weren't sure why she wanted us to wait, but waited nonetheless, just as she asked. Time went by, and we wanted to catch a taxi to our hotel, but she insisted we continue waiting. Finally, a couple of cars showed up, and she directed us into them. We were being given the courtesy of a lift to the hotel by our Chinese brothers in Christ, in gratitude for our delivery of Bibles.

By the time we got checked into our hotel, it was past 8 o'clock. We hadn't eaten since lunch, and we were starved. We met in the lobby and began walking the streets looking for food. At this hour, the restaurants were closing up for the night. We walked, and walked, and walked. Finally, Daniel, the young Frenchman with the Ph.D., asked in broken English, "Why not flag down a taxi and get a lift to a Kentucky Fried Chicken place?" It sounded so simple, once he articulated it. Daniel didn't say much, but when he did, it was important. We flagged down a taxi, and within minutes we were in a KFC ordering food. The rest of the team bought me dinner, since it was my fifty-fourth birthday. It had been a memorable one.

****

Another time, two of us had been sent to a secret warehouse inside China, one which is only used as temporary storage for Bibles. Our job was to pick up selected material and deliver it elsewhere. We had crossed into China with empty suitcases for this reason. My young buddy, Ben, was a professional cowboy from Colorado. We had taken the crowded underground subway. At the right stop, we exited and took the escalator upward, and upward, and upward some more, to eventually end up back on the surface. We wound our way through the maze of high-rise buildings to the right skyscraper.

Entering the lobby, we rode the elevator up to a high floor where we found the right flat and used our key to get in.

We had been given detailed instructions about where to find the right box and which Bibles to get for the upcoming delivery. We filled the empty luggage with the Precious Cargo, left the flat, and locked the door behind us. We retraced our steps back down the elevator and out the front door. We began to feel uncomfortably conspicuous as we crossed a wide, almost deserted plaza to the main street. Being Caucasian, we didn't look like anyone around us. Our anxiety level increased even further when we got to the red light at the crosswalk and set the heavy bags down. A motorcycle cop was parked right there, surveying the traffic as he sat on his bike. I watched him out of the corner of my eye, praying he didn't look my way and want to know what we had in the bags. I couldn't wait until we could get back down into the relative safety of the subway, where we could be lost in the typically huge Chinese crowd. Everyone there would be carrying some kind of luggage or briefcase. For once I was glad that China's subways are always so crowded. I felt like I had aged ten years when the light finally changed, and we got the walk signal. We crossed without looking back at the policeman, got onto the sidewalk, and calmly ambled the fifty yards to the escalator.

We breathed a sigh of relief as we went down and out of sight of anyone who might have been watching us. My relief quickly turned to horror. As we descended to the subway platform some seventy feet below, I saw something I never thought I'd see. The entire area was totally empty of people, except for one Chinese policewoman. She was standing at the bottom of the escalator looking up, watching us come down. This was about as bad as things could get. There was no way out. We went down, down, and down some more. As soon as we saw her, we looked away and pretended she didn't exist. There was nothing else we could do. We came down past her and walked over to wait for the subway, facing away from her.

Immediately she left where she had been standing, walked over to us and parked herself inches from my left arm. She stood staring up at me, waiting to be acknowledged so she could order us to open our heavy suitcases. She was young, slender, and stood about four-feet ten-inches tall. Physically she was no threat, but that wasn't the problem. She had a badge and a radio, and all she had to do was call for help, and we'd be facing a horde of irate Chinese police in no time at all. The seconds turned into minutes as she continued standing there, waiting to be recognized. We, on the other hand, faced the subway tracks, pretending we didn't see her.

I longed for the good old days of a few minutes ago, when we had been standing at the red light up on the street next to the motorcycle cop who never noticed us. Both Ben and I were praying fervently, "Lord, please hurry the subway. And if You don't want to do that, please make her go away instead of speaking to us." If she spoke, we would no longer be able to pretend that we didn't see her, and she would have every right to order us to open the bags. This is what they do, a part of their job. After what seemed to be several long minutes, she got embarrassed at not being acknowledged, so she turned and simply walked away. As I mentioned earlier, the Chinese really hate to "lose face." If she had spoken, and we continued to ignore her, she'd lose face. But she could save face by walking away and telling herself it was no big deal. Hallelujah! We were saved. We were still drenched in sweat when the train finally arrived and we could become less conspicuous again. Thankfully, it wasn't long until we were on our way.

****

Michael and I landed in a Chinese city of seven million people, carrying two hundred fifty Bibles between us. I was carrying about one hundred five, while he, being younger and stronger, was carrying the rest. The load was split between our backpacks and suitcases. We were met at the luggage carousel by our local contact, along with several members of the house church he pastored. We retrieved our suitcases carrying the Precious Cargo and followed them out to a van they had waiting. We said goodbye to some of our welcomers, but others climbed in with us. Along the way, we dropped off several more of them, continuing on with just our driver, who spoke excellent English. After a twenty-minute drive, we arrived at a high-rise hotel that seemed off the beaten path, but that wasn't unusual for this kind of work in China. We wheeled our heavy suitcases into the lobby and our driver/interpreter took care of checking in for us at the front desk. He mentioned that this was the first time our company had ever used this particular hotel. I thought it was odd. We usually stick with proven hotels, but I knew there might have been a problem with the previous one, so I didn't think much more about it.

As we left the check-in desk going toward the elevators, we passed by a couch where a couple of tough-looking characters sat glaring at us. I was glad we'd soon be safely in our hotel room with the door locked behind us. We got off the elevator on one of the higher floors and walked down the hall to our room. As we opened the door and turned on the light, hundreds of roaches, silverfish, and earwigs made a panicked dash for cover. Michael and I groaned, but there was nothing we could do about it. This was our home for the night. Our interpreter apologized and said he'd see us in the morning. I resolved to sleep on top of the covers, not wanting to see what lay under them.

There was a coffee pot, but no coffee or tea. No matter; it probably didn't work anyway. Walking farther into the room, we noticed a heavy mildew smell that we had missed when our attention had been diverted by the stampede of wildlife that shared the room. The bathroom door was closed. When I opened it, a sickening stench assaulted me; it was obviously coming from there. I tried to turn the fan on to get rid of the odor, but there was no fan, nor did the light in the bathroom work. At all. The smell was overpowering, so I backed out and closed the door. This was bizarre.

In between the twin beds there was a nightstand with a phone and a plaque which said, in both Chinese and English (kinda sorta, I guess), "For your safety please keep CHSH and valuable goods in head stage." Right, we'll get on that immediately. I took a picture of it for posterity.

At this moment, there was a deafening train whistle which lasted two full minutes. Looking out the window, we saw that we were less than one hundred meters from an enormous freight railway station. It was going to be a long night.

I badly needed a shower (Bible smuggling is hard, sweaty work), so I braved the smell and went into the bathroom. Did I mention the light in there didn't work? Well, there was no soap, either, or shampoo. I went back out into the main room to get my own soap, which was going to have to double tonight for shampoo.

This was really bizarre and getting more so by the minute.

I showered as quickly as I could and got out of there, shutting the door behind me, my nose burning from the mildew. About that time, I noticed that someone had stuck several business cards under our door. Stooping down, I gathered them up and took a look. Each one had a picture of a pretty girl wearing seductive clothing, and in both languages, it said something along the lines of "for a good time, call xxx-xxxx." Now it finally dawned on us. The tough guys in the lobby were pimps. Our missions organization had booked us into a house of prostitution for the night. We had a lot of time to consider all this, since the deafening train whistles continued all night long, making sleep impossible. Every few minutes, another train would arrive or leave. I reasoned that the engineer on every train must have been a neglected child and was determined to "be somebody" now that he had his own train. Even if it took honking the air-horn for long periods of time, well brother, no one was going to ignore him anymore. All night long, every time the whistle would stop for a few minutes, I could hear Michael muttering, "This place is a dump." The longer it went on throughout the night, the funnier his mantra became—to me, not to him. Even with all the misery, I managed to see the humor in it.

Next morning, I called my wife back in America to check in and tell her of our adventure. I hadn't gotten far into the story when, once again, a train blew its whistle. Trying to talk was useless. I had to wait for it to stop. When it finally did, I could hear her howling with laughter on the other end. She asked, "Has it been like that all night long?"

"You have no idea," I groaned.

That is the story of the time I called my wife from a Chinese bordello to say, "Hi Honey, guess where I spent the night?"

12

A Shift In Focus

In 2009, I had some vacation time coming, so I contacted Mary to see if I could book a smuggling trip. She said there were none coming up, but there was a trip to Bangladesh available, to encourage the persecuted Christians there. I declined, feeling I had nothing to offer God beyond being a pack mule. I was happy keeping things this way. I had seen a film clip once in which a pastor said that if you get up behind a pulpit, you'd better know something the congregation doesn't know, or there's no point to it. I was intimidated by the idea of encouraging believers who were going through things I couldn't possibly imagine. I needed to learn *from them*, not the other way around. Mary kept talking. Finally, I gave in, mostly because I didn't want to waste time sitting at home when I might somehow do some good in the world, although I couldn't imagine how.

I was to be on a team of four people going there. Although the persecution there isn't as severe as in many other countries, it does happen, and Christians are in the minority in Bangladesh. We went there to meet with the locals, hear their stories, and encourage them to stand strong.

I first became aware that this trip wasn't going to be business as usual when I switched planes in Dubai. When the time came to board the plane, the Bengalis swarmed past the ticket agent who was supposed to be checking them in. Evidently, this is common practice, since no effort was made to stop them. I waited in line like always, got checked in, and walked down the ramp to the plane. These Bengalis had evidently not flown much, because they had no concept of assigned seating. They were pushing and shoving to get into the plane door as if it were first come, first served. I was to find that this is just part of the culture. Bangladesh is the most crowded country in the world. In preparation for the trip, I learned that Bangladesh has more than one-third the population of the United States, yet the people are crowded into an area the size of Pennsylvania. Once on board the plane, the Bengalis were quickly reassured by the flight attendants that all was well, and they wouldn't have to fight for their seats.

Upon landing, I had to fill out the entry form, as is customary with entering any country. There were counters with stacks of the necessary paperwork. I picked up what I needed and began filling it out. There was no one around me when I began, but as I worked on it, the arriving Bengalis began to gather at the counter to do the same thing. The problem was, as more and more locals arrived, they filled the whole area and started elbowing me to move over. They did this instinctively, never looking up. They just filled in the blanks on the forms, all the while sliding slowly sideways, pushing me. When there was no place left for me to move because another guy on the other side was doing the same thing, I was forced to take a stand and shoved both of my elbows out. They are a small people, probably due to not having enough to eat during their formative years. I was much bigger than any of them, so when I stood firm, they backed off for the moment, but never really stopped trying to push when they thought I wasn't paying attention.

Once through Customs, I went to the baggage carousel. This was a whole new experience for me. It was a small area (not many people travel to Bangladesh), and as the conveyor belts moved the luggage in, some men were pulling the bags off the belt and stacking them in the middle of that tiny space. It didn't take long before the floor was jammed, and they began putting the new arrivals on top of the ones already there. The pile got higher and higher. I got there in time to see that mine wasn't buried under the stack, but as time went on and my bag didn't come out, I began to worry. Many other fliers were searching through the stacks also. Some of them were successful, some of them were not. The conveyor finally stopped, and my heart sank. I wondered which country my suitcase had gone to. I double checked all the ones I could see, but no luck. A taxi driver was retrieving a bag for his customer and saw me standing there. He told me not to worry. Sometimes it took six hours for them to get all the bags off the plane, but they usually turned up. I wasn't sure what to think about this, but I was happy when I finally saw the conveyor belt start again, and my bag came out in less than an hour.

The company I was volunteering with had a man waiting for me outside, holding a card with my name on it, a welcome sight. I had noticed a pretty young lady looking for her bags as I was looking for mine, and it turned out she was also part of the same team. Marleen and I bonded right off the bat, and she became "my South African niece." There were two other members waiting for us at the small hotel we would call home for the next five days. One was from Singapore and the other man from Brazil. We checked into the hotel and retired to our rooms to recuperate from jet lag.

Later, we met in the lobby and were taken to the home of the man who had met us at the airport, whom I will call Pastor Nathaniel. We were given an orientation about the state of Christianity in Bangladesh and were treated to a home-cooked dinner. When they served salad, I was hesitant to eat it. Remembering my ordeal in India, I knew the cardinal rule in all foreign travel is to never eat anything unless it's been thoroughly cooked. I was in a quandary, but I saw the others were eating it, so I joined in. Nathaniel had hosted Americans before, so I gave him credit for knowing how to make our food safe. After we were done eating, an argument broke out between Nathaniel and his assistant, in their own language. I could tell Nathaniel was upset, and the assistant was uncomfortable. Nathaniel turned back to us and explained that his assistant had bought the salad ingredients from a local outdoor market instead of the trusted grocer Nathaniel usually used. He apologized, but he couldn't guarantee it was safe. "Great, he tells us this after we're done eating," I thought to myself. Well, there was nothing to be done about it now.

Around 3:30 a.m. I woke up with a rumbling in my stomach. Half an hour later, I knew I was running a high fever. Soon after that I was vomiting. This wasn't my first rodeo, as the old expression goes. I had had food poisoning in India three years earlier. I knew what was happening to me. In India, I had been wiped out for several days due to eating a papaya which had been washed, after peeling, in the untreated water of the low-cost hotel where we stayed. Now here I was, nauseated with a high fever, and I only had five days in Bangladesh to serve the Christians. I didn't mind being ill as much as I minded the timing of it. Our first day of traveling around to meet the local believers was due to begin in a few hours, and I'd have to miss it, as well as probably the next two, if this was anything like my experience in India. I lay there burning with fever and had a talk with God. "I don't understand this, Lord. My life is yours, to do with as you please. But I thought You wanted me here, to encourage those who live in a land hostile to You. Now I've flown as far away from home as a person can get, to serve you and be Your hands and feet. I'd really love to be useful to you here instead of laying on this bed for the next few days. But Your will be done, however that works." Then I lay there awake, surrendering to God in the silence of my heart.

We had been told to meet in the lobby at 7:30. I decided I'd keep my eye on the clock and go down there when the time came to let the others know I couldn't go with them. They'd wonder why I wasn't joining them at the breakfast buffet by then, but they'd understand after I explained the situation. I looked at the clock on my nightstand. It was 5:20. I closed my eyes. When I opened them again, it was 7:20. I sat up to put my boots on. Suddenly, I realized that I felt great. I stood up. Yes, I was completely back to normal, or what passes for normal in my life. I hurried into the bathroom, shaved quickly, then grabbed my backpack, running out the door and down the stairs to the lobby. I hadn't been at breakfast with the others, and I knew I'd need some food to keep getting my stomach back to normal. I ran into the lobby where they all stood waiting for me. Setting my backpack down next to Marleen, I said I'd be right back. I ran down the hallway and around the corner to the breakfast buffet. I grabbed a napkin and filled it with several breakfast rolls, then ran back to the lobby, grabbed my pack and said, "Let's go." That was all they needed to hear. We were on our way.

As we drove out of the parking lot, I scarfed those rolls down, and they tasted oh so good. This was a miracle. I knew what should be happening to me right now, but instead, my appetite was normal. As I ate and watched the crowded city roll by outside the van window, the thought occurred to me, "People are praying for me, and this miracle is the direct result."

Dhaka, the capital of Bangladesh, is the most crowded city in the world. It takes hours to get a few miles across town. When a traffic light turns red and the vehicles stop, all of them pull to within an inch of the one in front of them. You may see the traffic light far ahead turn green, but not be able to move forward at all before it turns red again. This cycle will happen many times at each intersection. When you *are* able to move forward, it won't be long before everything stops again. Even if you're only going a few miles, it pays to only travel with people you like, because you're going to be stuck in the car with them for hours on end, with nothing to do but converse.

We needed to pick up a local colleague to guide us that day, so we drove to a rendezvous point and pulled over to the side of the road next to a busy meat market. Our friend wasn't there yet, so the driver turned off the motor, and we sat and waited. I watched the buyers and merchants haggling over the carcasses hanging from the meat hooks, with flies buzzing all around. My heart went out to those people as I thought of what their lives must be like, buying their food in places like that. I noticed there was a dog sleeping in the dirt below my car door. "He must be the most mellow dog I've ever seen," I thought. We drove right up to him, and he didn't even wake up. He must be used to all the cars constantly pulling in and out here, I guessed. After a while I got restless, so I opened my door and got out. Then I saw why the dog was so mellow. It wasn't a dog, exactly. It was only the front half of a dog. The rest was gone. Very likely, the rear half was hanging from one of those meat-hooks, covered in flies.

When our guide finally showed up, we left town and started moving through the beautiful countryside. We drove past numerous rice paddies until the road ended. We got out of the van and walked across the dikes between the paddies until we came to a tiny shack made entirely—walls and roof—of corrugated metal. We were met by a small family of Christians. The person we were there to see was a nineteen-year-old girl who serves as a "rural doctor" for that area. The company I was representing had paid six hundred American dollars for her to go to a six-month training program where she learned how to treat cuts, diagnose infections, and dispense antibiotics. The corrugated shack was her clinic and held the medications she used in her work. To an American, it might sound scary to trust someone so young and with so little training. But before she came, the nearest doctor was an hour's drive away, if you had a car. But no one here had a car, so a simple cut on the arm could be fatal if an infection set in. This nineteen-year-old Christian girl was saving lives. She lived with her sister and brother-in-law in a small shack behind her "pharmacy." Ninety-nine percent of her patients were either Muslim or Hindu. She was the light of God shining down into that region of rice farmers. We spent an hour with this precious young sister, listening to her story and praying with her, then walked back out to the van and continued our journey.

We traveled to a small town where we met with believers in their small house church. The pastor and his wife sang to the congregation of twelve believers, some of whom were his own family. They asked us to sing to them, so we sang "Amazing Grace," the only song our international team knew in common. As we sang, the pastor wept. The most difficult problem he has to deal with is a feeling of isolation. He feeds his flock spiritually but has no one to feed him. After we worshipped there, we gave him a lift over to a second house church he also pastors. This one had more people, about twenty. There were chickens pecking around the dirt floor inside the house, and the ever-present dogs were there as well. As one of the Christians was giving his testimony, a rooster began crowing, which made our team all laugh. But these Bengali believers just smiled tolerantly. To them, this was just business as usual.

On another occasion, our team was stuck in a meeting of Bengali pastors. I say "stuck" because the meeting went on for some time, and they were speaking in their own language, with no one interpreting for us. We each got bored and ended up doing our own thing. For myself, I opened up my backpack and took out my Bible. As I did, I got a clear message from the Lord, bringing to my memory the words of Deuteronomy 32:47. I wrote it down. A moment later, I received Philippians 2:14-16. Then a few minutes later it was John 6:66-68, then John 5:24. I wrote them all down. At that point, the spiritual telegram came to an end. I sat there a moment waiting for more, but it became obvious the message was finished. I looked at the list and realized each passage was referring to scripture as "words of life." I was amazed at how clearly orchestrated this had been. I had never experienced anything like it. I asked God to tell me what to do with this. I sat listening. Silence. All I could think of was that I was supposed to share it with my Bible study group when I got back home. I folded up the paper and stuck it into the pages of my Bible, putting it all back into the backpack. I thought of it several times in the next couple of days but didn't say anything to the other members of the team.

Two days later, we visited the graduation of a small seminary. Twelve young men had finished their schooling and were now going back to their villages to be ministers of the Gospel. We presented them each with a stack of books which all pastors should have in their library, in their native language of Bengali. Then the head of the seminary asked if any of us had a word from the Lord for them. Immediately, I realized why I had been given the list of scriptural passages, and I began calling out, "I do, I do!" The rest of the team watched me quizzically as I dug the Bible out of my pack, got the list, and began speaking to the students, connecting the dots of how all these scriptures fit together and would be the basis of their ministry from now on. I spoke confidently for ten minutes, with the seminary leader interpreting for me. Gone was the stage fright which had kept me from speaking to the congregations in India. Gone was the belief that I could do nothing but smuggle. Now I realized God could use me in any way He wanted, as long as I was open to His guidance. This was one of the most educational—and unexpected— events of my life.

One day, we interviewed four Bengali men who told us of persecution they had experienced. One man, a pastor, pulled the leg of his pants up to show me horrific scars on his shins, where he had been beaten with metal rods by men who were trying to get him to renounce Jesus. He never did, choosing to continue getting beaten instead. He spent a long time in the hospital as a result of the torture. I was reminded of Hebrews 11:25-26 (NIV), "He chose to be mistreated along with the people of God rather than to enjoy the pleasures of sin for a short time. He regarded disgrace for the sake of Christ as of greater value than…treasures…because he was looking ahead to his reward."

My smuggling trips had been tame compared to this. It was a whole new level of experience for me. I had read of this kind of thing, but now here it was in front of me. When each man had given his testimony, the pastor with the scars on his legs prayed for us as we parted company. Even though I couldn't understand his Bengali, there was no question about the power of his prayer. As he prayed, I knew the bells of heaven were being rung and angels were listening in respect. It was obvious my walk with God was anemic compared to this man. What did a spiritual wimp like me have to offer these people?

The five days in Bangladesh went quickly. One of my favorite parts of the trip was the final day. It was a conference where Muslim Background Believers (MBBs) were being given an orientation on what it means to live as a Christian. All of them had come to Jesus within the last year. This was the third year in a row that this conference had been necessary, since so many are coming out of Islam and into Christianity. There were more than a thousand MBBs in attendance. The conference was held in a beautiful setting of green grass and clean dorms where the MBBs stayed for the three days, courtesy of a Baptist organization. It was a fenced area to keep outsiders at bay and to give the MBBs the rare treat of being in an uncrowded, peaceful refuge. For those three days, they were given instruction on what the Bible is all about, from Genesis to Revelation. They were also told what to expect from their friends and family now that they had renounced Islam and come to Jesus. No punches were pulled; they were warned that serious persecution lay ahead of them.

Between the sermons, there were precious times of worship. These new children of the one true God worshipped with their whole hearts. We were introduced to them as visitors from other countries who had come to offer encouragement. Each of us gave a short greeting. Afterward, they couldn't get enough of shaking our hands and smiling at us. One man in his fifties took my hand, kissed it, and held it to his heart. I was fighting back the tears. Then he dragged me over to meet his grown sons. Now I knew why God had ordained this trip for me. I had almost backed out of it because I didn't see how He could use me outside of smuggling Bibles. Now I understood. I had thought it took talent to be able to give encouragement, but now I realized all I had to do was show up and reach out to these people in love and humility. All they needed me to do was to care. Seeing the new believers smile with their whole souls made those long flights and traffic jams all worth it.

The last morning, before dawn, Pastor Nathaniel drove Marleen and me to the airport. The sun was just beginning to make itself evident as he dropped us off, wishing us well. It was a building with five entrances, not unusual for a small country's airport. Oddly, though, each entrance was in itself a boarding gate, so we had to look at the departure screen outside the building to find our entrance and gate, number five. We walked down the sidewalk to the last door and went in. Appropriately, the security check was right at the door. An airport official came hurrying up to us and waved us out the door. He kept saying, "No, no, no," and pushing our luggage back outside the automated sliding door. I argued back, saying "Yes, yes, yes," and waving my paper tickets in his face. It was only two and a half hours before we were supposed to board, so we didn't really have time for bureaucratic nonsense, and I was rapidly losing patience with this guy who could only say no. We went through several rounds of "yes yes" and "no no." Eventually, it dawned on me that his English didn't go any further than that, so I decided to see if this was right.

I said, "Oh, you want us to go to another gate?"

He nodded and smiled. "Yes."

I said, "You want us to go to the wrong gate?" and smiled.

He nodded, smiling back and said, "Yes," in his deeply sympathetic way.

"You don't understand a word I'm saying, do you?" I said, still smiling.

He nodded again with his permanent smile and said, "Yes," drawing out the syllable. Then he added two more words which I was surprised he knew: "Half hour."

I realized something beyond me was going on here, so I let him push my suitcase outside the doors, and Marleen came with us, dragging her luggage. There was nothing to do but wait and see what developed. There was no one else around. We settled in for a long wait. Marleen kept looking anxiously at the departures board. She had to transfer in Dubai to catch her connection to South Africa. I was a bit more relaxed, having made arrangements to spend two nights in Dubai so I could tour the city.

A Bengali man came up with a suitcase in tow, only to be told, I assumed, the same thing we had been told. He was pushed back onto the sidewalk with us. Within the next few minutes, several more came to the gate with the same result. Another man came up, pushing a luggage cart piled three feet high with suitcases. He forced himself in between Marleen and me so she was on one side of the luggage cart, and I was on the other. The sun had fully risen now, and the sidewalk was getting crowded with irritated people wanting to get in and get going. Within half an hour, there were more than two hundred angry people on the sidewalk with us. Just when I thought it couldn't get any worse, an army truck pulled up, and a squad of soldiers jumped out of it. All eyes were riveted on them as they stationed themselves between the airport doors and the crowd. They pointed their assault rifles at our feet. Their sergeant had a discussion with the "Airport Official," the man who had pushed me out saying "half hour" more than an hour before. At one point, Airport Official pointed at me. The sergeant turned and looked at me. I wondered if Airport Official was saying, "Shoot him first," or "Don't shoot him, he seems nice enough." Marleen and I were right in front since we had been there before anyone else, but we were being pushed and shoved constantly by people struggling to get through. A few guys forced themselves to the front, so I pulled to one side and let them go by. They showed their paperwork to Airport Official, who seemed to be in charge of all this. They were firmly refused entry. So then they wanted to leave, but the crowd behind me was pushing forward even harder, making it useless for me to let them by to go back. Feeling victimized, they argued at me in Bengali as if I had some way of understanding them, and if I *had* been able to understand them, as if I could somehow do something, like maybe airlift them out of the crowd.

I got some humor value out of it, but in reality, there was no point in my trying to let them get past, because there was a solid wall of humanity behind me. There was no place for them to go. It was the same for the next one, and the next one, and....

I looked over at Marleen and saw she was really stressed. I didn't blame her. At this point, more than two hours had gone by, and it looked certain that she'd miss her connection to South Africa. A small man crowded into her with his cart, and she told him, "Stop, you're hurting me." I yelled at him to back off, jabbing my finger in the air at him. He didn't understand my English, but he got the picture from my angry tone, pulling back a bit, waiting for another chance to push forward.

I heard someone talking behind me and realized I could understand her. She was Bengali by appearance, but her accent was pure British. It turned out she lived in London and had come home to visit family. She was explaining the situation to a man next to her, who turned out to be Lebanese, but living in Florida. He owned a T-shirt business and was here to place an order for a large shipment of shirts. At this point, Airport Official addressed the crowd. Everything got quiet as he made his announcement. I was glad I had someone near me who could explain what was going on. When the man was done, my new London friend explained that all this fuss was because the president of Bangladesh was going to be on our plane. We were being held here until he was safely aboard. Shortly thereafter, the doors opened and the sergeant in charge of the soldiers waved Marleen and me forward, ahead of the rest. We were finally on our way.

When we finally landed in Dubai, Marleen wanted to give me a farewell hug, but it was already late for her to catch her connecting flight. We were also on different sides of the aircraft, so I called out to her, telling her to run like the wind and try to catch her next plane. I found out later she did make it. A deep friendship was born during those five days. Years later, when my wife and I did another missions outreach to South America, Marleen found out we were going to be there, so she signed up for the same trip. We had a wonderful reunion and spent the week together working at a children's home there.

From the airport, I took a taxi to the hotel I had booked. Dubai is an interesting place. The vast majority of the workers there are from poverty-stricken countries. They are only allowed to stay in Dubai as long as they have a job. If they get laid off, they have thirty days to find another job. If they can't find one, they are deported back to their home country. A sign on the back window of the cab had a phone number and urged the rider to call with any complaints about the driver. The taxi was the cleanest I ever saw, and the driver was the most helpful and polite as well, needless to say.

I checked in to the hotel and had a nice dinner in the restaurant on the ground floor. From a lobby-office, I booked a city tour for the next day. The level of culture shock was immense, after spending the week in Bangladesh. I had gone from perhaps the poorest country in the world to one of the richest.

The next morning, I was picked up in front of the hotel by a bus full of fellow tourists. The tour was all I hoped it would be. Dubai is an artificial city. Everything has to be brought in from other countries: the food, building materials, clothing, furniture, workers...everything. If their supply lines were cut, everyone would die. But as long as their oil keeps flowing, they can keep paying people to bring supplies in, and they can stay afloat.

As the bus took us down a freeway, I saw an off-ramp sign which actually said, "No camels." I couldn't get my camera out fast enough to take a picture, much to my regret. I can only guess that sometimes people ride camels on the freeway, and it's enough of an issue to warrant putting up a sign.

I had an enjoyable day seeing the sights and listening to the Japanese tour guide explaining all the details of the city and how it functions. Back at the hotel, I ate a sumptuous dinner, still thinking about those people in Bangladesh. I slept well, got up, and packed after breakfast. As I left for the airport I thought, "Wow, I'm feeling a little rumpled." At the airport, a friendly Muslim ticket agent gave me my boarding pass. She asked if I'd like to sit in the emergency exit-row so I could have more foot room. I was impressed by how sweet she was, and I knew that with a long flight ahead of me, I'd be a lot more comfortable with the extra room. I didn't know it at the time, but it was also right next to the toilets, a fact which would soon be of great importance.

I was feeling worse and worse now. I had a window seat, so I was able to use a pillow against the side of the plane to rest a bit and close my eyes. Suddenly, I was freezing cold. I asked the man next to me if he had ever been on a plane that ran the air conditioner this low. He was confused by the question and said he wasn't cold at all, that this was how all airplanes are. I thought he was crazy; this was clearly wrong. Then, even more suddenly, I had to make a run for the toilet. Thankfully, no one was occupying it at the time because I seemed to have been struck with dysentery. That was the norm for the whole flight. My bowels were in an uproar, then vomiting began. When I finally landed in San Francisco, I had a fever of one hundred three degrees. Fortunately, it was a weekday, and I was able to get right in to see my doctor. I spent the next five days on antibiotics before finally beginning to come around to normal again.

At some point it dawned on me. I had gotten sick on the first full day of ministry in Bangladesh, but God had pushed the "pause" button on the illness. I thought I had been completely healed, but now I realized He wanted me to see exactly what I had been healed from. He had kept the illness at bay until the work was finished. He even gave me a wonderful side trip after the work was done, letting me see Dubai. Then after the great gifts, He pushed the "play" button, and I got to see how my week would have gone without His touch. I ended up being grateful for the whole experience, because I got to see it from His perspective. And He was so gentle with me that He even saw to it that I got extra leg room and a seat right next to the toilet.

His hand had been on me the whole time, caring for me.

13

Learning to Trust

After a few years of hearing the stories of the great people I had met and all the adventures I had while smuggling Bibles, my wife decided she had to see all this for herself. I contacted my source of trips and told her that Donna would like to accompany me on one, if it wouldn't be too dangerous. Not long after, we got the assignment to make a delivery to a country in North Africa. It wasn't as bad as some, but the Christians there couldn't get Bibles on their own. So, we made plans.

We flew into Europe and spent a couple of days seeing the sights before meeting our contact to pick up Precious Cargo, which we would then smuggle into our destination country. We spent a wonderful afternoon of Christian fellowship with them, getting the rundown for the country where we were headed. It was middle of the road as far as persecution goes. No Christians had been killed there in recent times, but a church had been burned down a few months before our arrival, and Bibles had been forbidden there for many years. To me, it was business as usual by now, but Donna was nervous. She loved to travel, no question, but she wasn't comfortable with the potential danger. I was proud of her for going outside her comfort zone to serve God in this way.

During our orientation in Europe, we were told that Al Qaeda was kidnapping Americans in this country where we were headed.

Another warning we got was that for every uniformed police officer we saw, there were nine more undercover we wouldn't see…hopefully.

We packed the "presents" into our bags, divided between our backpacks and the suitcases. As international trips go, this was a short flight, from our European staging area to the repressive Muslim country. Short in hours of flying time, but eons different in terms of lifestyle. During our five days there, I took a picture of a sign outside a shop which advertised horse meat for sale. Yep, we weren't in Kansas anymore, Toto.

We deplaned and got in line to go through Customs. I had been through this enough times to know I just had to give it all to God and keep myself in a zone of prayer. That was why I missed a lot of what happened in the next few minutes. Donna was all eyes, praying intensely also, but watching to see if we were going to be arrested or…something worse.

After clearing Customs, we moved to the critical phase, going through security. It has always been paradoxical to me that in American airports you have to go through metal detectors and x-ray machines to get on an airplane and leave the country, but in the airports of developing countries you get searched when leaving the plane to enter the country. Trying to take some of the pressure off Donna, I went first. I put my backpack on the conveyor belt, which immediately took it forward into the x-ray machine, disappearing from my consciousness. I took everything out of my pockets, took my belt off, my shoes, etc., then went through the metal detector and around to pick up everything I had just taken off. It wasn't much different from going through security to fly out of San Francisco Airport.

As I was getting myself put back together, Donna came up to me vibrating with excitement. "Did you see that?" she asked in an excited whisper. I hadn't, so she told me the story. As my backpack went into the x-ray machine, a well-dressed businessman carrying a briefcase jumped out of line and barged through the metal detector, setting off alarms. Security officials came running from all directions, and a shouting match ensued. One of the first guys to run toward the businessman was the guard who had been watching the x-ray machine. My backpack sailed through with no problem. By the time Donna had taken everything out of her pockets and put her pack on the conveyor belt, the guard had come back to the x-ray monitor. As her pack entered the machine, he walked up to his stool and hit a button, stopping the conveyor. As she stood there petrified, the guard was approached by one of his colleagues. They stood there talking for a minute as time stood still for Donna. As he finished the conversation, he hit the button, starting the conveyer again, but he didn't look down until Donna's bag had gone past the monitor. I had seen this kind of thing many times myself, but this was the first time for her. No matter how many times you see this, it just never gets old. God always comes up with new variations of the miracles which make this type of ministry possible. It made me smile to see her have this experience.

We went over and picked up our suitcases from the luggage carousel and steeled ourselves for the next part of the journey, going outside the terminal to look for our hosts. While picking up the Bibles in Europe, we had asked for information on who would be meeting us. They had no idea who it would be. The underground Christians just use whoever is available on the day they are needed. As we found out later, our reception committee hadn't been told anything about us, either. They didn't know if it was going to be two older folks, two young folks, two men, two women…nothing except that it would be two people. They depend on the Holy Spirit to guide them. That way nothing can go wrong. Wow, talk about learning to trust God.

There were multitudes of people already streaming out the front of the terminal before us and many more coming out behind us. Yet as soon as we walked out the door I saw a man who nodded to me as our eyes met, then turned to say something to a partner behind him. Then he turned back and pointed to me. I knew beyond all doubt, this was our brother, sent here to meet us. I spoke over my shoulder to Donna, "We've been picked up." She told me later she didn't know if that meant we were being arrested or being met by friends.

She said, "How do you know?" My mind went over the many different ways to answer her, all of which would take me several minutes to explain, none of which I had the time to go into right now. All I could do was move forward in the moment, then explain it to her later when this was done.

"I don't," was the reply I finally settled for. That calmed her down…not so much. Our new friend left the place where he had been waiting and came down to the barricade which separated the waiting people from the new arrivals. He walked along on the outside of the barricade, and I paralleled him on the inside of it for some thirty meters before it ended, and he came up to me.

"Do you know Mike from Switzerland?" he asked. I shook my head no. "Do you know Ahmed?" he asked,

"No," I replied. Then, in French, he gave me the name of the organization which had sent me. I nodded with a smile, which he returned.

"We are here for you," he told me. My wife still calls this "the miracle of Mustafa" (not his real name), since he picked us out of the multitude of arriving passengers, without having to think about it. He was shown by the Holy Spirit, as he told us later.

We followed our new friends out to the parking lot. Mustafa spoke pretty good English, but our driver spoke none at all. Mustafa began giving us a rundown of the country as we left the airport parking lot. We could see the capital of this country in the distance, where we were supposed to be staying, but we were headed in the opposite direction. Donna was alarmed, but we had seen too many miracles in the last hour for me to doubt that these guys were legitimately our people, regardless of which direction we were headed. One thing I've learned on these trips is that seldom does anything go as planned. It had become part of the charm of this kind of adventure. As combat soldiers say, "No battle plan survives contact with the enemy."

I've been to many repressive countries around the world since beginning this kind of work, but this country had a new twist. The repression isn't directed just against the Christians but is designed to sift out the terrorists and bandits which are so prevalent there. Every few miles, we came to a roadblock which didn't bring us to a complete stop but forced us to slow down to a crawl and drive in a semicircle around barricades before picking up the road again on the far side. As we negotiated the slow crawl, there were soldiers every few yards holding their Kalashnikovs (assault rifles) at the ready. As our car drove by each one, they peered into the windows, examining us. According to our hosts, this practice has been in effect for many years. It was an eerie feeling knowing we were carrying Bibles in the trunk, and that these guys with the guns would freak if they knew we were Americans. We passed through checkpoint after checkpoint like that, every few miles, for the three hours it took to reach our destination city.

Arriving there, we were driven through ordinary city streets with American-looking traffic lights and paved roads. We entered a neighborhood where we came to a two-story building inside a compound which had a sliding-gate eight feet high. Mustafa told us to stay in the car until we were given the "all clear." He spoke on his cell phone, and a moment later the gate was pushed open by someone on the inside. Our car pulled in, and the same man pushed the gate closed behind us. At this point, we were given the "all clear" to get out of the car. Later, we found out this well-known Christian compound is under constant surveillance by the police.

Mustafa told us to not bring our luggage, since we would not be staying here during our time in this country. We followed him up some stairs and into the house, which turned out the be the living quarters of the pastor and his family. We were introduced all around and spent the next few hours getting to know the pastor, his wife, and our two guides from the airport. Later on, several more people came in, and we met two German men who had been there all week and were now on the way to the airport to return home. As it turned out, one of the Germans and I had heard of each other by reputation, and we had many stories to swap, of places we had both been and people with whom we had both worked. When we were first introduced, he had been gruff and distant, but after a few hours of telling each other the many miracles we had each seen, he gave me a bear hug and a wonderful smile when he and his partner had to leave for the airport. It's been a fun part of this ministry that it's a small world. It's not unusual to run into the same people from one trip to another; if not that, then you find that you have friends in common from previous trips. Not many westerners do this kind of ministry.

We were treated to a tasty Arabic meal, the kind of thing you don't get in Americanized restaurants at home. I ate hummus for the first time and many other dishes I didn't recognize but enjoyed. When the Germans left for the airport, we also left to go to what would be our home for the next five days. It was a safe house for Muslims who have accepted Jesus. The converts' families invariably kick them out (or worse), so it's common for the local Christians to take them in and give them a safe shelter where they can be discipled further along their journey. Our host was a former Muslim man I'll call Hassan. Mustafa couldn't join us, since he had a full-time job there in the city. We'd see him later in the week when we got together for worship.

When it was time to go "home" for the night, we were driven up a hill where there was no pavement, but there *was* a forest of sophisticated-looking high-rise buildings. It was an odd contradiction: the modern high-rises amid the dirt streets. When we got out of the car, Hassan led us into the nearest high-rise, then took us up many flights of stairs in total darkness. These modern-looking buildings had no elevators, nor any working lights in the stairwells. Hassan would go up ahead of us and flip open his old-style cell phone, which would activate the light, and he'd hold it behind him to illuminate our climb. When it timed out and turned off, he flipped it closed and back open again, repeating the process all the way up seven floors. Once we got to the door, he opened his phone for the last time and called his wife to open the door for us. That was the only way anyone got in. If anyone knocked on the door, it was a dead giveaway that it wasn't someone who belonged there. This is a common practice in many persecuted countries; I saw it time and again. In many cases, there is no doorknob at all, just a deadbolt on the inside. So there always has to be someone at home. It's a safety system which works well.

Once inside, the apartment was nicely put together. There was a television and modern refrigerator, stove, and toilets. The one odd thing (for us) was that there was a limited amount of running water. To bathe, we had to fill a bucket with water and sit in a tub, using the water to sponge bathe. For us, it just added to the adventure.

During the five days in this Muslim country, our time was spent being driven from house church to house church, speaking with the pastors and their laymen. We listened to their stories and heard of their hardships. All the Christians we met were former Muslims. Almost all of them had come to Jesus as a result of having dreams or visions. We only met two who had converted because of someone witnessing to them. It was fascinating that no two of them had identical stories. God gave each one of them a unique experience tailored exactly for them.

We were slow to catch on to the fact that our hosts would be in serious trouble if they were found to have Americans in their homes. The first inkling we had was on our arrival at the main pastor's compound, when we were told to stay in the car until the huge rolling gate closed behind us, so no one could see us. We really didn't think much of it at the time; we just obeyed to be polite. But the next day on our trip around the area, we had to stop in a local neighborhood for about half an hour. Our driver and our safe house host were both elders in this underground Body of Christ, and the driver needed to make a house call. One of the believers had lost her mother, so he was called in to pray with her and offer scriptures of comfort. We sat in the car for that half hour with our guide keeping us company—and keeping an eye on us for our protection, as it turned out. The neighborhood was beautiful, with many yards having flowers I had never seen before. I asked our host if I could get out and take some pictures of the flowers. "No," was all he said. I still didn't put two and two together at that point. Eventually, it all sank in.

During our time there we were never allowed to speak with anyone outside the church community. We were never allowed to order our own food nor get any local currency, despite my hobby of collecting paper money from around the world. We weren't allowed to buy anything on our own or go anywhere by ourselves. When we left in the morning, we never knew where we were going or when we'd be getting back.

The kicker was when the main church held a big weekday service. Some two hundred fifty believers showed up. They sang loudly to the accompaniment of electric guitars. The preacher used a microphone when he preached. It was a house church all right, but one on steroids. Over the years, it had been remodeled numerous times. Inner walls had been removed leaving a good-sized main room. We were ushered in and seated against a back wall. Our host apologized quietly, explaining that they would not be able to introduce us to the congregation. They would have loved to do this for us, but it was known for certain there were informants within the group. If they announced Americans were present, someone would send a text, and within a few minutes the police would come surging through the doors, and many would go to jail. As I watched the people sing enthusiastically of their love for Jesus, I scanned those faces I could see, and I wondered which of them were informers. The risk certainly didn't intimidate the former Muslims, now Christians, into downplaying their commitment to the one true God.

One of the things I have loved most about this kind of work is seeing all the different ways God can be worshipped. For instance, in this church, when they celebrated communion, a large glass basin was filled with wine and passed from person to person. Each one took a sip and passed it on to the next one. Then a large loaf of bread was passed; each person took a pinch and passed it on.

The need to remain anonymous became all the more poignant late one night after we bid our hosts goodnight and retired into our bedroom. Donna held out her hand for me to inspect. When I looked, the whole world stopped. Earlier that day she had reached deeply into the trunk of the car to get her jacket at one of our stops. She felt something bite her thumb near the wrist. It left a distinct puncture wound, but she said nothing at the time. She monitored it through the day as it swelled up, and a red streak began traveling up her wrist onto her arm. Now that we were alone, she could show it to me. Instantly I began to consider our options. We could tell our hosts, but they couldn't take us to a hospital without revealing that they were harboring Americans. That would certainly land them jail. We could try to walk through the city and find a hospital on our own. The odds of finding one were practically zero. Even if we were able to locate a hospital, the doctors would call the police. No, we had only one viable option: pray.

So, with the intensity of desperation, I prayed: "Father, we need You as badly as anyone has ever needed you. This is really, really bad. We are totally in Your hands here. We need a miracle. Father, in the name of Jesus, we ask You to heal Donna right now. Right now. We can't go on without Your divine touch. We ask this in complete faith that you will heal her. Amen." It wasn't a long prayer, but it didn't need to be. I was talking with the Creator of the universe, who already knew the whole situation and who loved us so much that He had sent His Son to shed His blood on the cross. We had already seen so many miracles on this trip and heard of even more, so I knew beyond any doubt, God was healing her right then. He had allowed this to happen to show His power and love to us in this situation. I was so certain of it, I took a picture of her wrist, so we could show people in the years to come the evidence of God's miracle—how He had manifested His presence in our dire situation. After praying, we felt so peaceful that we went right to sleep and slept well all night. In the morning, the red streak had stopped right at the place it had been when I prayed, and it was beginning to fade. The swelling was going down, too. By the time we got back to the States, the wound was barely visible.

This was a turning point in Donna's life. From then on, she understood what it meant to trust God. I'm not saying He always heals our bodies. He doesn't always. But we can be certain that He will either heal us physically or give us the spiritual strength to continue living in His peace through it.

Donna had always been afraid of standing up in public to talk. At our baptism, when the pastor asked her to give her testimony, her lips moved but no sound came out. Now, the day after her healing, I woke up to see her staring at the ceiling in silence. When I asked how she was doing, she responded, "I'm great. I'm just putting together the presentation I'm going to do for our church when we get home." She proved to be as good as her word. Not long after we returned home, she gave one of the most polished talks I have ever been privileged to hear. She has never been the same since she went on this trip and saw God in action with His persecuted children.

As we were driven around these mountains to visit the house churches, we noticed we never traveled the same route twice. Each journey was a loop so as to avoid arousing suspicions by the gendarme. They might suspect something odd was going on if they saw us twice. Also, we made sure we were off the mountain roads before dark, since bandits are common in these parts. It was sobering: we were in danger from the government, from vigilante Muslims, and from bandits who didn't acknowledge allegiance to either of them.

In one town where the persecution is heavier than the others nearby, we met with a pastor and two of his elders. His congregation of about a hundred meets openly, despite knowing the locals are opposed to them. One of the elders has been unable to find a job because he's a Christian. He's been out of work for two years, with no relief in sight. Yet, the pastor brimmed with joy in spite of all they are facing. He told of an old man who frequently stations himself across the street from the church to make them uncomfortable. Whenever the pastor comes out of the church, the old man holds up his cell phone and tells him, "I can have you killed with just one call." The pastor responds to him in love, trying to engage him in dialogue, but the harassment continues.

We spent five days in that country during which we visited ten house churches. In each one, we asked them how we could pray for them. Every church requested us to pray that they would stay strong in the Lord regardless of the hardships. Not once did they ask for God to make their lives easier. They know what the Bible says about living under hardships in this world and being rewarded when Jesus is revealed. After we left, we had no way of keeping in touch with them because they are under such heavy surveillance. We think of them often with fondness and keep them in our prayers. They have set us a great example of standing strong as they trust in God.

14

Dembidollo University

In 2012, there was an outburst of violence against Christians in Ethiopia. Fifty-eight churches were burned, as were the houses of twenty-nine Christian families. Within six weeks of the end of hostilities, a team from the company I volunteered with was on the ground to comfort the believers who were traumatized. In a crisis like this, it's crucial to follow up later with additional teams. I was on a team of nine people sent the next year to be that follow up.

Flying out of San Francisco, I changed planes in Istanbul. Before leaving home, I had been contacted by one of my fellow travelers who was coming from Amsterdam. She emailed me to say we'd be on the same plane from Istanbul to Ethiopia, so we should look for each other at the departure gate. Once I got there, it only took a few minutes to pick her out of the crowd and introduce myself. Anna turned out to be a valuable part of the team, an intrepid and experienced traveler who spoke three languages.

We flew into the capital, Addis Ababa, and were picked up at the airport by the local head of the missionary company. We loaded our suitcases into the back of his van and climbed in. As we drove through the night, the scenery reminded me of news reports I had seen of African war zones. The dark, deserted streets were unpaved, and many of the buildings appeared damaged and deserted.

We arrived at a hotel which was protected by a ten-foot high concrete wall running all the way around it. Stopping at a massive gate, our driver made a call on his cell phone, a dangerous country's version of ringing a doorbell with which I had become familiar. A few minutes later the gate was opened from the inside, and we drove through. It was closed and locked immediately behind us. I was glad to see these people took their security seriously.

Once inside the compound, the whole atmosphere changed. The grounds were beautifully landscaped, and the hotel would have done justice to any hotel in America. I checked in at the front desk, got my room key, said goodnight to the others, and went upstairs. Jet lag is always an issue on intercontinental travel. I was glad to crawl into bed, under the mosquito netting which hung from the ceiling.

Sleep was elusive, partly due to the jet lag, but also because of the oppressive heat. So, I was wide awake when I began hearing interesting animal noises from outside my window. I watch a lot of nature shows about Africa, and I realized immediately that there were hyenas right outside my room. At first, I couldn't believe it, but there was no mistaking that sound. Nothing else sounds like hyenas. They were hunting for prey on the streets of the largest city in Ethiopia. I was thankful for the big wall around the hotel which kept the real Africa out. I suspected that there weren't many homeless people living on the streets of Addis Ababa. They wouldn't survive for long out there.

The next morning, the hotel staff confirmed that, yes indeed, there *were* hyenas roaming the streets last night. In fact, they're quite common on that side of the city.

The team assembled in the hotel lobby, and we introduced ourselves to each other, shaking hands all around. That was always one of my favorite parts of any trip, the first morning when no one really knows the other team members yet, but we begin with shared excitement for the days ahead. On this assignment, we had members from France, New Zealand, South Africa, England, Holland, and another teammate from the U.S.

We had seen our itinerary before leaving home, and the plan was to use small planes to hop-scotch around the country to the places we needed to visit. Ethiopia is a big country, and we needed to cover a lot of territory. There were a number of towns we needed to visit where churches had been burned. Our schedule included visits to two widows whose husbands had been hacked to death with machetes, simply for being pastors. One of the widows had also had a son killed just a few months earlier when a grenade was thrown into a house he was visiting.

At that point, our itinerary changed drastically. Just days before we arrived in the country, Sudanese terrorists had crossed the border and killed a busload of nineteen Ethiopian men on their way to work, right in the area where we were headed. We still needed to get there to meet the Christians who were hurting, but the government had shut down all domestic airports. So instead of flying, it was necessary that we travel in a convoy of three Toyota Land Cruisers. Our main destination was a place called Dembidollo, just a few miles from the border with Sudan, where we were to meet the first widow. Our purpose was to hear her story, pray with her, and deliver a host of support letters which had been written by people from all over the United States. One batch of those letters had been sent by a discussion group led by my wife, Donna. When her group had written those letters of encouragement back home in California, I never dreamed I'd be the one privileged to deliver them.

We had some downtime that first full day after our orientation, so I used it to get caught up on sleep. Our second morning in the country, we were on the road by 8 a.m. It would take us two full days of driving over dirt roads—bouncing, I should say, distantly related to driving—to reach Dembidollo.

We stopped after a few hours and visited a congregation whose church had been burned the previous year. We heard the stories of their suffering and of the horror of the attacks. In this case, the worshippers had been in the church when the Muslim mob came howling in off the road with their torches blazing. The Christians fled into the jungle in back of their church and spent the next two days cautiously making their way to the nearest town, without food or water during the whole journey. Once there, they reported what had happened, and the police mobilized quickly to stop the attacks and arrest those responsible. The church had been rebuilt now, and we worshipped with our brothers and sisters in their new sanctuary. It was constructed of eucalyptus branches, and the cracks were sealed with a special mud they use in their construction. The best part of the story was that the believers had responded to the attack by loving their enemies instead of seeking revenge. The result of their Christ-like attitude was that three Muslim families had been so touched, they gave their hearts to Jesus and joined the church.

We got back on the road a few hours later. As we crossed a bridge over a good-sized river, our driver matter-of-factly announced, "Hippos." I didn't understand at first, thinking it was some kind of joke. But as soon as we had reached the far side of the bridge, he pulled the Land Cruiser over and turned off the motor. We got out and walked to the middle of the bridge, and sure enough, there were a number of hippopotami down below us calmly enjoying the river. We took pictures and marveled at the sight, but soon a young man with an AK-47 came out onto the bridge and ordered, "Taking pictures is forbidden." Of course, I walked around behind him and took his picture to capture the moment. Then we piled into the Toyotas and got back on the road.

The countryside amazed me because it looked exactly like the part of California where I lived. It would have easily passed for the low hills around Gilroy with brown grass and trees. From a distance they looked like oaks. The big difference was that there were beautiful black and white monkeys in these trees.

Another thing unique to Ethiopia is the farms which grow eucalyptus trees. We were told the story of how someone long ago had imported five of them. They became the mother trees. Eucalyptus only take three years to grow big enough for use. They are harvested and cut into usable lengths. The Ethiopians use eucalyptus for everything from houses (filling the cracks between the logs with the specially mixed mud) to scaffolding and even wheelbarrows. I took a picture of a man pushing his eucalyptus wheelbarrow down the street.

Before long, I noticed something among my fellow teammates who had traveled Africa before. When they were done with a bottle of water, instead of tucking it away in a garbage bag for later disposal, they'd wait until we drove by a group of people. Then they would roll down the window and toss the bottle out into the group. The first time I saw this, I couldn't believe my eyes, thinking either they were being disrespectful by throwing garbage at the people or were simply trashing the countryside. But as I watched, a mad scramble ensued to get the bottle. What I thought of as garbage, in my American mind, was a treasured canteen to Ethiopian people who had virtually nothing in the way of worldly goods. There were water wells all along the roads we traveled, many drilled by charities from America and Europe to provide drinking water for these people. But wells don't do them any good unless they have something in which to carry the water. Each household had a big yellow five-gallon jug for the family, but there was also a need for more portable canteens, and these half-liter bottles were perfect for the job. We could benefit poor people wherever we went, just by passing on our empty water bottles.

We stopped the first night in a mid-sized town and stayed in a hotel which was much better than I had expected—at least better as far as cleanliness. But I soon found that air conditioning didn't exist in Ethiopia except for the wealthy, which didn't include us. We sweltered in the stifling hot rooms. We were grateful that we had a roof over our heads, mosquito nets above the beds, and walls to keep out the hyenas. It was even better that my room was insect-free. We couldn't expect more than that. This turned out to be the norm; every hotel room was as hot inside as the weather was outside, but without a breeze to make it bearable.

We ate a tasty buffet dinner and a decent breakfast the next day. Our Ethiopian guide, Jacob, knew we were heading into an area where the available food was unsafe for foreigners, so he bought a large quantity of croissants which would end up being lunch, dinner, and breakfast for the next few days. Most of us also carried snacks in our backpacks, so we were not overly inconvenienced.

Before leaving the hotel to continue our journey, Jacob introduced me to a young man in his early twenties I had been hearing about for months. He had come to Jesus not long before. His angry family, who were Ethiopian Orthodox, had beaten him severely, tied him up, and thrown him into the back seat of their car. They were in the process of taking him out into the country to "kill him for God" when a police officer spotted them. Something made him suspicious, so he pulled them over. When he walked up to the car, there was the young man all trussed up, lying in the back seat. The father of the family proudly told the cop their story, expecting to get support for what they were doing. But the cop turned out to be an evangelical Christian. He rescued the young man. Now he had been given refuge by other Christians and was attending a seminary to become a preacher. My wife's discussion group had written letters to him, which I carried in my backpack. Jacob arranged for him to be driven to our hotel, where I presented all the support letters to him personally. He was overwhelmed, never thinking anyone outside the area knew his story, or cared. Jacob translated some of the letters to the young man, as he sat on the couch with a huge smile.

On that same day, as we got closer to the Sudanese border, we were stopped at a military roadblock and ordered out of the vehicles. The soldiers did a thorough search of the cars and our luggage, evidently looking for weapons. It was likely a response to the terrorist attack we had heard about. The soldiers were not destructive, thankfully, and once they were satisfied we were the good guys, they let us get on our way.

Later, we stopped one hour short of Dembidollo to visit another congregation. We met the pastor, heard the testimonies of the believers, and prayed with them. The driver of my Land Cruiser grew more and more agitated as our time there went on, and he finally told Jacob we really needed to hit the road because it would be dark soon, and we still had far to go. He was chomping at the bit to get moving. Jacob finally agreed, so we loaded into the vehicles and set out for Dembidollo.

Before we had been on the road five minutes, a heavy rain began, along with thunder and lightning. The road was slippery, but our driver went faster instead of slower. We were sliding around every curve in the road and bouncing over each straight section. As I studied the driver's face, it dawned on me that he was afraid of something. I asked him where the danger was. Was it in trying to negotiate the bumpy dirt road with his headlights in this rain? After a long pause he answered, "No...it's the night." Finally, I understood what the problem was. He was frightened of being on the road after dark, afraid the terrorists who killed the nineteen men on the bus (close to where we were at this point) might still be there, and they might kill us, too. It was a sobering realization, and I began to pray that the rain-slick dirt road would hold together long enough for us to get to Dembidollo. Thank God, we arrived in one piece an hour later, just as it got fully dark. The rain became a heavier monsoon.

As we exited the vans, Jacob had a word with us. "Not all the rooms have showers," he told us. "Okay," we said. After all, this is remote Africa, and we can deal with that. Those who have showers can share with those who don't. No big deal.

We checked into the "hotel," then found out the rest of the story. None of the rooms had any running water at all, despite some of them having the plumbing in place. Half of the rooms had no toilet of any kind, let alone a shower or sink. Those rooms were simply four unadorned walls and a ceiling. Even the rooms which had toilets didn't have any toilet paper, which didn't matter anyway, because as I said, there was no water. Here in malaria country, this was the first place we stayed which didn't have mosquito netting over the bed. To top it all off, the bathroom window of my room had no glass in it. If all that weren't enough, five minutes later, the power went off, not to come back on until some time the next day. So, the one light bulb in the center of the room became an annoying decoration.

I went back outside where one of our group had begun ranting at Jacob. He just stood there with a patient, gentle smile. The guy delivering the rant was telling Jacob there was no excuse for not having toilet paper. I thought this was hilarious, since half the rooms didn't even have toilets! The lack of bathroom tissues was really the least of our worries. The angry man was using phrases like "no excuse…reprehensible…should have known." The hotel owner stood behind Jacob listening but not understanding the rapid English. Finally, Jacob turned to him and translated. The owner replied angrily. Jacob turned back to the complainer and translated what the owner had just said: "He says this is the best hotel in town, and if you don't like it, you can check out of here and go stay in the second-best hotel. And I have to tell you, I've seen the other one. He's right. This is by far the best." Through it all, Jacob never lost his sweet smile, and by that point I was laughing at the whole situation.

A crowd had gathered to listen to the exchange. When the furor over the toilet paper was finished, Jacob told us apologetically that there would be no dinner tonight, since the places which had food were so filthy, the food wasn't safe. Ah, I do love adventure travel.

After taking my gear into my room, I went back out to watch nature's extravaganza. Rarely have I seen such a spectacular display of lightning. There was an open area up on the second floor where several of the others had gathered under an overhang, so I went up and joined them for the show.

Twenty minutes later Jacob came around to gather us together and told us he had found a safe place to eat, after all. We piled back into the Land Cruisers and drove five or six blocks. The whole town was pitch dark with no sign of electricity anywhere. Our convoy turned down a lane, proceeded a few more blocks, and then came to a halt. Jacob got out of the lead vehicle and walked back to our car to say, "We're here."

I climbed out into the torrential downpour and looked around. We had parked next to a building, and it seemed to be part of a neighborhood, but all the houses were dark. I asked, "Where is 'here'?"

He pointed forward and replied, "Go up to the corner, then downhill to the left."

One of the key items on our trip checklist had been a flashlight, and it really came in handy there in Dembidollo. I followed my flashlight beam to the corner and peered down a steep muddy road. I realized at that point why the Land Cruisers had stopped instead of taking us all the way to the restaurant. If they ventured down there, they wouldn't be able to get out until a few days after the rain stopped and the road had dried out. The mud was ankle-deep. I could see no sign of life down there, no light at all, but I followed the directions. I slipped and slid, then slipped and slid some more, for more than fifty yards, stopping occasionally to turn off the flashlight and see if there was any sign of life. I could hear the others coming down behind me, but I didn't want to wait for them. I wanted to get out of the heavy rain. All around me, there was only complete darkness. Finally, *finally*, some seventy-five yards into this muddy foray into the dark, I spied a light off to the left, and it turned out to be an open doorway. When I got near, I clambered over a small embankment of mud, into the entryway of a house, and found that this was indeed our destination.

A local Christian family was trying to get a business going and had set up their house as a restaurant. The front room was large and had been turned into a dining room. My fellow travelers arrived one by one behind me, taking off their muddy shoes as I had done, then entering in stocking feet. In the dining room, there were three tables-for-two, and then a long table set up for us, so we could all eat together. Cooking was no problem on this night of no electricity, because they did all their cooking over wood fires, just as they did every day. They treated us to a delectable traditional Ethiopian dinner, paid for by the missions company which had brought us here. The family had candles set up for light adding greatly to the ambiance. It was a night I'll never forget—for the food, the fellowship, and for the adventure of getting there.

After dinner we clambered back up the hill, slipping, falling in the mud, and finally making it back to our chariots.

Back at the hotel, I had a sudden suspicion, remembering other places I had stayed on previous trips. So before getting into bed, I got my flashlight ready, then quickly jerked up my pillow and shone the light under it. When I did, a multi-legged creature scrambled out from under it and scurried under the sheets. I slept on top of the covers that night, with DEET sprayed heavily on all exposed skin. Since my window had no glass, I prayed, asking Him to be my protection against malaria. "He's better than mosquito repellent, anyway," I thought. I remembered Psalm 20:7 (NIV), "Some trust in chariots, and some in horses, but we trust in the name of the LORD our God." The Ethiopian version of this verse would have read, "Some trust in insect repellent, some in malaria pills, and some in having glass in their windows, but we trust in the name of the LORD our God."

Next morning, we woke up to bright sunshine, with no leftover rain clouds. We drove farther into the town of Dembidollo and met with the widow whose pastor husband had been killed in the machete attack. Her six children had come with her. They ranged in age from a toddler to a sixteen-year-old son. Normally, she had to walk six hours to get to town. But on a rare occasion like this, someone had driven part way out there to where the dirt road ended, picking her and her family up so they wouldn't have to walk the whole distance. Getting to meet her was an unforgettable experience. She hugged us and hugged us, kissing us on both cheeks until I thought she would never stop. It meant so much to her that people from so far away cared enough to come to see her. As we introduced ourselves, Jacob instructed us not to go into much detail about where we were from. She had no concept of different continents or oceans. She may not have ever even seen a television. Her life consisted of hard farm work, raising children, and being a pastor's wife. Now she was a pastor's widow.

We spent about ninety minutes with her. Jacob translated some of the letters I had brought for her, and the women of our group prayed with her. Even two years after her husband had been killed, her emotions were still raw. She struggled to make ends meet, even with the missions company helping her. Seemingly undaunted by their plight, her sixteen-year-old son wanted to be a doctor, and her fifteen-year-old daughter wanted to be a preacher, just like her dad.

We departed around noon to head back to Addis Ababa. On the way, we stopped for a break in a small town which had an outdoor coffee shop. As we sat sipping our coffee under awnings which kept the hot sun off, we became the afternoon's entertainment. People would walk by on their day's business, look over and see us, then come to a complete stop, speechless at what they were seeing. They seldom saw white people, if at all. In no time, there was quite a crowd of gawkers. They were not hostile, just shocked, and they weren't shy about staring.

I walked out away from the coffee shop to get some pictures of the town, and an older man approached me, clearly wanting to be friendly. He wore an American-style baseball cap and even knew some English words. He asked, "Where from?"

We had been told these folks had no concept of world geography, so I simply responded, "From far away."

He smiled shyly and tried to make sense of it. Then he queried, "From Nekemte?" Nekemte was the next city along this road, and he really couldn't conceive of anything much farther in his whole world.

I didn't want to confuse him, so I just said, "Even farther than Nekemte." He shook his head in amazement that anyone could live in far away regions beyond Nekemte. We smiled at each other, and he let me take his picture. We shook hands and went our separate ways.

Later, as we drove through another town, we had to stop for a funeral procession. I've never seen anything like it. There were a couple hundred women all dressed in white, walking together. All traffic stopped in respect. This was one of the rare times I didn't take a picture. You never know when photographing mourners in other cultures might seem disrespectful and result in violence.

When we stopped for the night, Jacob took us to a restaurant near our hotel. I had learned the hard way that the food in Ethiopian restaurants is dangerous. Two members of our group had already gotten food poisoning, one of them being me. As I said before, I knew from my water treatment classes that if food is heated to one hundred eighty degrees, all harmful bacteria will be killed. So, one way to be safe in developing countries is to order pizza, which is usually cooked on the spot and gets hot enough to be safe. The eatery Jacob took us to this time offered pizza. This made me happy. But when Jacob ordered for me, the cultural experience began.

The waiter asked him a follow-up question. "Do you want cheese on your pizza?" Jacob interpreted. I didn't understand the question, so I asked for clarification. Jacob repeated, "Do you want cheese on your pizza?" I was obviously still confused, so he went on to tell me that cheese isn't normally put on Ethiopian pizza—but I was told that they were out of cheese anyway, so it didn't really matter.

Baffled, I said, "Okay, make it without the cheese." What I got was bread, half an inch thick, covered in vegetables. It was huge too, two feet in diameter. It was almost big enough to feed our whole group without anyone ordering anything else. There was indeed no cheese, just lots and lots of vegetables. It was well cooked, however, and none of us got sick.

After two days on the dirt roads, it felt good to get back to Addis and have an evening's rest. It was nice to be able to kick back and recharge my emotional batteries in clean rooms. After what I had seen during the previous few days, this hotel felt like a Hilton back in America. And, of course, my old friends, the hyenas, were back, serenading me as I fell asleep under the mosquito netting.

The next day, we headed south on paved roads to visit more Christians who were living under persecution. Our primary focus was to visit the second widow, but we were also going to make the most of our time by visiting another community which was under attack. No matter where you go in Ethiopia, there is serious persecution going on, so we had no lack of options.

Every few miles, we saw women and children lined up for water at the local wells. They all waited patiently with their yellow five-gallon jugs. This is a basic part of every-day life for them. In the morning, they walk for miles to the nearest well. Then they have to carry the heavy jug all the way back home for the family. Five gallons of water weighs more than forty pounds. It's the same routine again in the afternoon. The men work the fields and care for the livestock; the women gather firewood and take the kids to stand in line to get their water.

Arriving in a large town, we proceeded through the neighborhoods, stopping in front of a compound made from high walls of impenetrable cactus. The gate was opened from the inside, allowing us into a large garden next to a small house. This was where the second widow lived with her six remaining children. She was the pastor's wife I mentioned who had lost her husband to Muslims with machetes, and who had recently lost her twenty-one-year-old son when someone threw a grenade into the house where he was visiting with other Christian friends. What I am about to share is one of the saddest things I have ever seen. This precious woman sat on the couch with her children around her, with an expression of exhausted despair, mostly looking off into the distance as we shared scripture and prayed with her. We were just a nuisance she had to put up with in order to get outside help for the family's basic needs. Her kids were typical kids, laughing and enjoying the change in their routine. They had exotic company come visit them. These children had seen so much tragedy, yet kids the world over are so resilient. Nothing can keep them down for long. Unfortunately, none of their excitement rubbed off on their mother. She was inconsolable. She and her family were forced to move from place to place frequently out of fear of being found and facing even more violence. Local Christians did what they could to see that the family was provided for, but they still didn't have much. We left her place with heavy hearts.

Back on the road, we drove several more hours, stopping at a local outdoor market to buy more bottles of water. After storing them in the backs of our vehicles, we turned off the paved road and drove many more miles on nicely passable dirt roads. Thatched huts lined both sides of the road, with people watching our convoy from their doorways. It wasn't every day they saw motorized vehicles come down this road.

My Land Cruiser was the last in line of the three. I need to explain that our drivers weren't Christians; evidently, they had been hired for the journey because there were no Christian drivers available. We came to a crossroads which was, as I later found out, a consistent trouble-point. I heard our driver mutter under his breath in English, "I hate being last." I couldn't understand what his problem was at first, but I soon found out.

There were two young men standing beside the road where it exited the intersection. I thought nothing of it at first, but our driver held back from following the first two vehicles as they moved on along the road without us. He honked his horn and waved at the young men to back away from the road. But there was no movement from them. They stared at us indifferently. The driver, more agitated now, motioned vehemently at the older boy. Finally, he stepped back in resignation. The younger kid was about fifteen years old. The driver spoke harshly to him in their language, and he came closer to the Land Cruiser, just out of reach. The driver and the kid spat words back and forth a few times, and then the kid laughed at him. The driver eased the Land Cruiser forward cautiously. The boy approached the driver's rolled down window, and our car stopped. With no warning, the driver suddenly reached out, grabbed the boy's arm and pulled him violently in, slamming the teenager's head against the roof of the car. As the teen recoiled in pain, the driver gunned his car forward. There was a flurry of motion behind us, as other teens came bursting out from behind bushes and rushed the back of the car. They were a tad late, and we got away quickly.

When I mentioned this episode later to more experienced Ethiopian travelers, they educated me. It's widely known that missionary groups who come to this area are well supplied with food, water bottles, blankets, and much more. I've never heard of anything like this before or since, but evidently, these cars are the economy version, and the back doors don't lock. The teens have learned to attack the last car in any convoy, opening up the back doors and plundering what they can before it escapes. I was in shock by how the driver had bashed the kid's head into the car, but evidently, this is how the non-Christian drivers get their job done. These two had evidently had numerous encounters previously and knew each other well. What the driver did wasn't right, but it seemed to be a predator/prey encounter peculiar to Ethiopia.

Fifteen minutes later, we drove through a gate into a fenced area where there was a school building. Our missionary company was teaching more than five hundred local children to read and write, as well as do basic math. The students were overwhelmingly Muslim, but there were some Christian kids as well. There were only two classrooms, so the students were divided into morning and afternoon sessions.

After greeting the two rooms full of students, our group began walking the half mile to the large thatched hut which served as the local church. As I walked beside our local Christian guide for this area, I finished off the bottle of water I had been carrying. A small boy had come up and was walking along beside me. I thought back to how we had been throwing our empties into groups of people as we drove. I asked our local leader if it would be all right to give this boy my empty bottle. He nodded, so I turned and gave it to the kid. I've never seen more happiness in this world. His face lit up, and without a word, he turned and ran out across the field we were paralleling. Looking ahead of him, I saw he was running toward a well where a long line of people stood with their big yellow jugs, waiting their turn at the pump.

We came to a community of thatched huts built close together, with the largest one in the middle being the church. As we filed in, we saw the congregation was waiting for us. The hut was round so the benches had been placed in a circle around us. We were introduced to the believers, and several of us got up to share scriptures with them. Then four of them stood up and told their stories. These four were called "the evangelists." They live in the church full time. Every morning, they split up and head in different directions to spread the Gospel. One of them bears a scar that runs from his forehead, down across his nose, and continuing down onto his cheek. While evangelizing, he was attacked by Muslims with machetes. They left him for dead, but God had other plans for him. As soon as he was mobile again, he was right back out witnessing.

Our Ethiopian leader for this part of the trip told us that the week before we arrived, a family in this church had had their home burned down by Muslims. In addition, another family had had two goats stolen just the night before. To Americans who get their food from large grocery stores, this might seem inconsequential. But to Africans who eat or barter what they grow, it was like taking food out of their refrigerator or money out of their bank account. A stark contrast to these stories of hardship came when they treated us to singing and traditional dancing to honor us. This congregation was rejoicing even in the midst of their persecution.

Our drive back to Addis Ababa was bittersweet, since we knew we'd be flying home the next day. We had our last meeting that evening, all of us reliving our favorite parts of the trip. When we added up the kilometers and did the conversion to miles, it turned out we had covered 1,405 miles in those Land Cruisers. This trip was so impactful to me that when I got home, I had two T-shirts made which said "Dembidollo University." I felt like I had been given a full university education during that week.

I had one last night of sleeping in the sweltering heat as my friends, the hyenas, serenaded me one final time.

15

Lion's Den

I was given the assignment to "deliver" Bibles to a radical Muslim country where the level of violence was off the charts, against Christians, yes, but also between Muslims. I had to sign a confidentiality agreement before I left, requiring me to never tell where I had been on this trip, ever. I didn't understand just how serious that was until I got there and saw how much the Muslims in this country hated Christians…and Americans. This country is so dangerous that when the trip coordinator asked me to go, she apologized to my wife, who happened to be nearby at the time.

One of the biggest obstacles in making this trip was finding a partner to go with me. All of the experienced people I knew simply answered with a decisive no. The level of hatred for Americans was so high there that none of the "old pros" would even consider it. I was different because I truly felt called to do this kind of work and saying no would have been the same as telling God no. I had refused His commands too much in my early life. It had led to so much heartbreak that I would never refuse again. The missions company had allowed me to go alone once before to Istanbul, when I couldn't find a partner. After I got home from that trip, I received an email from Mary which had no comment, simply a link to a news story. It told of a murder which happened right after I came home. A Muslim in Istanbul had decided one day that he was going to kill a Christian for Allah. So, he waited outside a church until the service was over, then stabbed to death the first person to walk out the door. Point made, I'd never be allowed to go alone again.

Finally, the trip was about to be canceled for lack of a partner when a name came to my mind. I have a pastor friend in Benicia, California, who is a great man of God, and who is absolutely fearless. When I put the question to him and told him to think about it overnight, he replied, "I don't have to think about it. Yes, I'll go with you." I called Mary and told her not to cancel; the trip was back on.

Mike and I flew out of San Francisco Airport. My wife drove me to the airport, and I arrived there before him. I secured my boarding pass and checked my suitcase through to the European city where we would be picking up the Bibles.

Mike's wife dropped him off a bit later, and we met at the boarding gate for our flight. He related that when he showed his paperwork to the ticket agent, she was quiet for a moment, then said, "In all my years of working here, I've never issued a boarding pass for that country."

We flew to the airport in Europe, retrieved our suitcases, and took a shuttle to the hotel we had reserved for the occasion. After checking in, I texted my local contact, who brought the Bibles to us in our hotel room. He had wrapped the Bibles with Winnie the Pooh gift paper to make them look like gifts for children. But I was concerned about the quality of the paper. It was so thin that it tore if you weren't extra gentle with it. Even packing my backpack was too rough, and some of the paper tore, exposing the Bibles inside. I prayed God wouldn't let this be an issue, that He would get us in without my suitcase or pack being searched.

Our contact gave us an orientation for the country we were flying into. There were fewer than forty known Christians in the whole country, despite its size. This was sobering. He also told us that on one of his trips there, he flew to an airport hub. When he attempted to transfer for the final leg of the journey, his flight was delayed because an armed militia had taken over the destination airport. He was stuck for hours before there was a resolution to the situation. After he finally reached his destination, he found out from the locals that the situation had been resolved when a much larger militia showed up. They were expecting something on an incoming flight, and this standoff was bad for business. So, the smaller band had to leave the airport or die. Quite effective bargaining, I thought.

The plan was that upon arrival, we were to be met by a man named Abdul (not his real name). I didn't think twice about it because on all previous trips like this, I'd been met by someone who used to be Muslim but was now a serious follower of Jesus. Abdul was to take us to our hotel, then in forty-eight hours he would pick us up and take us back to the airport. We had been told not to take a taxi under any circumstances. Getting into a taxi would mean our deaths. The people in this country passionately hate Americans.

Between us, Mike and I were carrying twenty-eight Bibles. It wasn't a huge load as this kind of work goes, but given the level of danger, we didn't want to push the envelope too much. At least this small load was manageable. I tried to get them all into my pack, since some nations only focus on the suitcase and allow the backpack to bypass the x-ray machines. This time there just wasn't enough room in my pack. I stuffed in as many as I could, then had to put the remaining ones into the suitcase.

The next morning, we caught a shuttle over to the airport. I had to laugh as the radio in the shuttle bus played Kenny Loggins singing "right into…the danger zone." There could not have been a more appropriate song for what was to happen that day. We checked our suitcases in at the ticket counter, and soon made the short flight to our destination. Once we landed, it didn't take long to clear Customs, but it was nerve-wracking just because of where we were. I watched the Customs agent examine my passport carefully, stamp it and hand it back. Thankfully, there was no problem, but the hard part still lay ahead. As I walked away toward the luggage carousel, a uniformed man came up to me and asked, "Diplomat?" It was a legitimate question, since no one travels to this country unless they are government people or news reporters. I shook my head no, and he gave me a puzzled look before walking away. I thought he must be waiting for someone specific. There weren't likely to be any other Americans on this plane.

Mike and I met at the luggage carousel and waited for our suitcases. It didn't take long. Mike's came out first, so I told him to go ahead so it wouldn't be too obvious that we were together. One rule of thumb in this kind of work is that if you have two lines to get in, you split up and make use of each one. That way, if the first guy gets caught, he won't draw attention to the second person. It will just appear that the one guy was traveling alone. Mike went first and took the left line, so I got into the right one (which also turned out to be the wrong one). The x-ray monitors were the largest I had ever seen, the size of big-screen televisions. In China and Vietnam, they had been small nineteen-inch models. These were huge because it was an oil-rich country, and they spared no expense to scan all incoming luggage.

I was happy to see no one sitting in front of the x-ray monitor for my line. The suitcase went right through, and I was singing in my heart with gratitude as I went around to the far side of the conveyor belt to pick it up. Pulling it off the conveyor belt, I set it down, extended the handle, and began to wheel it away when a young man came running up to the monitor, took a look and then yelled at me to stop. He was about twenty-five years old and wore the uniform of airport security for this country. I had no choice but to stop and see what was next. My heart began trying to jump out of my chest and get away on its own. The agent pointed at a table nearby and spat Arabic words at me. I didn't have to speak his language to know what I was supposed to do. There are always tables near the x-ray machines in restricted countries to facilitate their jobs of searching suitcases. I rolled the suitcase over to the table and put it up on top. The security agent came over and spat more words at me as I dialed the combination on the luggage lock, took it off, and unzipped the bag, opening it up as he watched. There, to my horror, were several of the Bibles. They had been tossed around in the suitcase, and the wrapping paper had torn making it obvious what they were. The guard picked one up and examined it, running his fingers over the words on the cover. He did the same with a second one. Some of the packages hadn't torn open. Several of them were wrapped in larger bundles, two Bibles per package.

He turned and called out to an older man who was nearby, wearing the same security uniform. That man stopped in the middle of what he was doing and came over immediately. The younger man showed him the torn package and the Bible. Then they went together over behind the huge x-ray monitor. The older man sat down, disappearing out of sight, and the younger man bent down next to him, also disappearing from my line of vision. Now I had time to think as I stood there, my heart pounding and my hands shaking. As I stood there waiting for the next development, I thought, "I'm going to be undergoing torture in less than half an hour." Needless to say, my mind was on God and my need for Him, but no actual words of prayer came across my mind. I knew the words wouldn't matter, regardless. The Lord knew my heart, and my heart was crying out for rescue. My silent attitude of supplication was all the prayer I had or needed. Either God would rescue me out of this or give me the strength to let my suffering be a witness, if that was His will for me. I found out later, seven people were praying for me at that precise moment. Donna and Mike's wife had each set their alarm clocks so they could wake up and pray for us; the others woke up in the night thinking, "Darvis is in trouble," and they began calling out to the Lord for me.

The younger security guy stood up from behind the x-ray machine and came back over to me. He went through my whole suitcase, rummaging around and finding all the packages. He picked each one of them up and ran his fingers over them, as if by touching the edges he could figure out what kind of books they were. Surprisingly, he didn't tear the packages open, although he had all the authority in the world to do that. He carried one of the double Bible packages, which hadn't torn, over to the older security man and once again disappeared down below my line of sight, behind the x-ray monitor. More time went slowly by. Finally, he brought the package back. He dropped it into my suitcase and returned to his behind-the-monitor conference with his boss. There was nothing I could do but stand there praying earnestly. After I had been standing there for the longest ten minutes of my life, the younger man raised up above the monitor, deep anger on his face, and growled, "You can go" in English. To this day, my wife can make chills go up my spine by growling "you can go" at me, just as a joke.

I tried to keep my head and look nonchalant. Reaching down to close the lid on my suitcase, my hand was shaking so badly that I actually missed the zipper pull, landing an inch to the left. I felt like every eye was on me, and I didn't want to call any more attention to myself than I had to, so I resisted the urge to pull my hand back and try again, knowing I'd likely miss it the second time as well. Instead, I left my hand on the edge of the bag and slid it along until it got to the zipper, grasped it, then pulled it closed. Pulling the suitcase off the table, I set it on the ground and walked away praising God for yet another delivery from the lion's den.

As I walked out the terminal door, Mike was standing there with the man who turned out to be our driver, whom I assumed was Abdul. Mike explained that this wasn't him, but this guy worked for

Abdul. Fair enough. Mike had sailed through security with no trouble at all and had been waiting for me outside the baggage area.

On the way out to the car, we passed the money exchange. We needed to exchange some of our dollars before leaving the airport, so I asked the driver to wait a minute. I pulled out my wallet, stepped into line, and prepared to make the currency switch. Before I could get up to the exchange window, I was approached by a local who held out a wad of rolled up money and motioned at me to come with him. I looked at our driver and said, "Is this all right?" He nodded, so I followed the man with the money roll. We just walked a short distance away, where he stopped and pulled out a calculator. He didn't speak English, but he didn't need to. I looked over at the official currency exchange window where there was a brisk business being done and wondered what was going on here. I looked back at our driver, who was watching me calmly. Mike and I looked at each other, not knowing for sure what to do with this. Was it a con of some kind? I indicated to the money-roll guy that I wanted to look at some of the money and he handed me some bills. They looked legit to me, but really, how would I know how to tell the difference in this country? I held out the amount of money I wanted to change, and he figured it out on his calculator, then held it out for me to see the number. I looked over at the official numbers shown at the government exchange and did some figuring. Americans get conned in foreign countries all the time, so I was really looking at all the angles here. How did this guy come to be doing business this way? I didn't have a lot of time to think it through, but our driver seemed unconcerned, so I took a chance and moved forward with the deal. I gave him American dollars, and he gave me the local currency. Then Mike went through the same process. Only much later did I come to the conclusion that the underground banker had been dealing with stolen money. Whether he had robbed a bank, embezzled it, or robbed an arms dealer, clearly this was a criminal enterprise. In these countries where there is constant upheaval, I'm sure this is common. It was just that I had never seen it before.

We followed our driver out to his car and loaded the bags into the trunk. Then he drove us through a bombed-out city to our hotel. From the back seat, I took pictures of scores of bullet-riddled buildings, including what was left of a stadium that had been bombed into a useless concrete mess. It was a half hour ride to our hotel. Once we got there, I was pleasantly surprised to see that it appeared to be in good shape, although the wall across the street was pockmarked with what looked like fifty-caliber bullet holes. There were buildings all around us which were still standing and were obviously still occupied, but few of them had escaped being shot up. Many were missing glass in their windows; many were festooned with graffiti depicting armed fighters in combat.

We checked into the hotel in the same way we would have checked in anywhere else in the world. This seemed odd, considering the condition of large parts of this city. I reluctantly handed the desk clerk my American passport. I would have preferred to remain silent and be taken for a European, a much safer prospect here. "Adventure travel," I thought to myself.

There was a working elevator to take us up, and our room was surprisingly fancy. I would have been happy with these accommodations anywhere in America. This was far better than I had hoped for. There was even a working restaurant in the hotel lobby.

I dialed the phone number I had been given and spoke the assigned code phrase to the person who answered. They had been told where we were staying and said they would pick us up outside the hotel the next morning. Since it wasn't safe for Americans to be strolling the streets, we kicked back in our room until it was time to eat dinner.

The restaurant downstairs wasn't fancy, but it wasn't bad either. As we ate, a man approached us and offered his hand, saying in perfect, unaccented English, "Hi, I'm Abdul." This was the man we had expected to meet us at the airport. He sat down and began making polite conversation, schmoozing like a salesman playing his customers. He was a native of this country, but he had lived in the U.S. for many years. He had emigrated to America when he was young enough to learn to speak English without any hint that it wasn't his first language. He had owned a business in the United States, but after 9/11, his business had gone under, since no one wanted to patronize a shop owned by a man named Abdul.

The friendly mood quickly turned sour when he informed us that we owed him money—and told us how much. We knew we owed him, since he was the one who had "fixed" it for us to get visas. Without his help we would have never gotten into this country at all. We had been told by our European contact that Abdul would be charging a certain amount, and included in the price was the agreement that he'd be taking us back to the airport in forty-eight hours. Our contact had also told us to make sure to get a fully itemized invoice for the agreed-upon price. But now Abdul was padding the bill significantly and refusing to give us any receipt. Not only that, he was refusing to take us back to the airport unless we paid an outrageously higher amount. He was blackmailing us, knowing we'd get killed if we took a taxi. He figured he had us over a barrel. It became obvious at this point that we weren't dealing with a Christian brother, but with a Muslim black-marketeer.

We had been instructed by our home office how much money to bring, and not to bring an ATM card, given the likelihood of it being stolen (translation: the likelihood of us being robbed). At times like these, I am prone to react more on instinct than clear reason, which can be dangerous. It's one of my worst faults.

I looked at Abdul and said, "Ain't happening." He replied that he wouldn't be taking us to the airport, in that case. I said, "Fine." Mike and I each handed over the amount he was demanding, minus the blackmail amount for the lift to the airport. We realized that Abdul could easily have us killed for the money. In this country, it's almost a hobby for some of these guys. Abdul said thanks, then stood up and said goodbye. I didn't know what we'd do for a lift to the airport, but I knew God was in control. I thought back to Psalm 31, one of my life verses: "I trust in you, O LORD…my times are in your hands."

The hotel restaurant overcharged us for the meal, but we only realized it after we had eaten. So, we had no recourse but to pay the bill. I was annoyed. As we left the restaurant, I noticed Abdul was still there in the lobby, so I went over and asked him if there was any other place to eat, thinking of the next night. He told us to follow him and he'd show us a Turkish place which had good food, and where the owners were friendly to Americans. I would never have gone outside on my own, but I really didn't want to eat here in the hotel again. And since we had a local guide, we followed him out into the night. As we walked, Abdul regaled us with stories of all he had seen since he left home at age fifteen, and how indestructible he was. I got tired of it quickly, but if he took us to a place where it would be safe to eat, it'd be worth it. After we had walked about a mile, we happened upon a clean, friendly place where the owner spoke English. Abdul introduced us with smiles all around. I looked at the menu and recognized the Turkish flatbread pizza I had come to love on my Istanbul trip. I was satisfied. I told the proprietor we'd be back the next night, and we said goodbye to Abdul and parted company.

We walked back to the hotel and spent the rest of the evening in our room, hunkered down. The next morning, our local brothers met us on the sidewalk right outside the lobby just as they had promised and took us to their congregation. We delivered our Precious Cargo, to their great delight, and we worshipped with them for hours. It was a wonderful day of fellowship. After church, they treated us to a great feast, and I don't know when I've eaten better. As we sat chatting after dessert, I asked the house-church pastor if it would be safe for us to take a taxi to the airport the next morning. His eyes went wide in alarm. "Absolutely not. We will pick you up in the morning and take you there. Do not take a taxi, it would be very dangerous for you." He would be as good as his word the next morning. Thanks be to the Lord!

After the exotic meal, they took us back to our hotel. Since we had never been in a country this radically bad before, we didn't take into consideration that it was Friday, the Muslim Jummah (which literally means "gathering"). On this day, they worship at the Mosque, and for several hours all activity in the city comes to a stop during the holy hours. The Muslim observance of Jummah on Fridays is similar to the Jewish observance of the Sabbath on Saturdays. When our hosts dropped us off back at the hotel, I remembered that I needed a couple more bottles of water. I could see a shop of some kind down an alley not far from where I stood. Crossing the street, I went down the alley a short way, and sure enough, there was a shop which carried bottles of water. I went in and walked to the cooler where the bottles were kept cold, but the proprietor waved me off, pointing at his watch. Then I remembered about everything shutting down for a while on Fridays. Okay, I nodded to him. I'd come back in a few hours. Many "conveniences" aren't available during those hours.

We walked into our hotel and pushed the button on the elevator. The door opened like always, giving us no warning of what was about to happen. We stepped into it and turned around, looking out into the lobby. Two hotel employees sat on a couch right next to the front desk, watching us with sullen scowls. Yep, I was thankful we had brothers coming to give us a lift to the airport tomorrow. These people truly hate Americans. I pushed the button for our floor, and the elevator doors closed. It just sat there, going nowhere. I waited a bit, then hit the button for the third floor again. Nothing. At this point, it dawned on me that the Muslim day of prayer affected elevators too, and I realized we were stuck until it was over, but I had no idea when that would be—sundown or much later. I knew those two guys sitting on the couch were just thirty feet away, and they knew their customers were stuck in this elevator. I pushed the emergency button, which resulted in a loud ringing bell. I let it go after a few seconds. Nothing. So, I hit it several more times intermittently. Nothing. I thought, well, if they're sitting right there, I'm going to disturb their harmony. I pressed the button down and just held it. One minute, two minutes. I finally realized that the more I pushed the button, the more I made them smile. I wasn't disturbing their harmony; I was giving them entertainment. So, what to do now? I had never forced elevator doors open before and didn't really think it was workable. Mike, on the other hand, wasn't about to be deterred and said he'd take the bottom if I'd work the top. So we both began trying to force the doors open. I stuck my fingers into the crack between them and pulled with all my might. He was doing the same down below. With a lot of effort, we were able to get them a quarter inch apart, then work our fingers deeper for a better grip. With that added grip, we were able to get them a half inch open. At that point, we were able to get our whole hands into the opening. Straining with all my strength and Mike doing the same, I was finally able to get my elbow into the gap and gain enough space to work my shoulder in. I did a kind of pushup, using one door as if it were the floor and my back against the other door. At that point it became easy, and we sprang ourselves out of the trap. Our two wonderful hotel friends were still sitting on the couch glaring at us in hatred. "No, no, don't get up. We're good, but thanks anyway," I told them. We walked up the stairway with them drilling holes in our backs. "Better stares than bullets," I thought to myself.

We hadn't been back in our room long when we heard a loud explosion. Mike and I looked at each other and wondered how bad this would get. In war-torn countries like this, the windows are usually the type which can be opened by pushing up. Since there was no screen, I lifted the window and I stuck my head out to see what I could see. I looked in the direction of the main street (our hotel fronted on a side street) where there was a sidewalk espresso shop with several tables. About half of them were occupied by Arab men enjoying their day of rest. I had expected to see people running to get away from danger, but no one seemed to be concerned. As I watched, a number of shots rang out. All of this noise seemed to be coming from around the corner, just out of my line of sight. One or two of the men at the table looked in that direction but went back to their coffee. Evidently, this was just another day in paradise for them.

We sat down and talked over the morning's adventure for a while. Presently Mike said, "I could do with a cup of coffee." I leaned out the window again. All seemed calm, so we put our shoes on and walked down the stairs past our friends still sitting on the couch. It was a short walk to the end of the block. As we walked, I glanced up at the high rise on the next block over with many of its windows shot out. Sights such as this had come to seem like a normal part of the landscape of this city.

Crossing the street, we walked up the three stairs and entered the shop. The proprietor understood us well as we each ordered espresso coffees. Then we went out and picked a table. A few minutes later, the barista appeared with our drinks and set them in front of us. The cafe was situated on a corner of an alley, and I noticed that there was a cartoon spray-painted on the side of the building just across from where we sat. I couldn't resist getting up and taking some pictures of the caricature of their currently out-of-favor leader, made to look like a fool by this graffiti artist. As I took the pictures, one of the locals walked by and began passionately explaining its meaning to me, pointing at it and speaking in rapid-fire Arabic. I pretended to understand and nodded my head in sympathy for all that had happened here in his beleaguered country.

Shortly after I returned to our table on the sidewalk in front of the coffee place, there was another huge explosion from around the corner, and car alarms began going off. The boom came from the same direction as the previous blast and gunshots. I prepared to run—or what passes for running with my disabled leg. It was only a couple hundred yards to the front door of our hotel. As I got ready to hit the sidewalk, I looked around at the other coffee drinkers. Some were looking in that direction, but others were simply gazing off into the distance or into the bottom of their cup. Two women came walking by, one pushing a baby in a stroller. I relaxed a bit and sat back. The day was hot, in the nineties at least. I took another sip of my coffee. Every few minutes, there were more shots and the occasional explosion, accompanied each time by the car alarms which were set off. No one ran or even looked stressed. I could only surmise that there must be some training in progress, and that this was just an everyday occurrence.

Eventually, we finished our coffee and we walked back to our semi-refuge. Having learned from our elevator adventure, we took the stairs this time. We spent the rest of the afternoon in our room, safely ensconced, swapping stories. Mike had been a rock musician back in the sixties, in his B.C. days, and he had some great tales.

When it came time for dinner, we retraced our steps back to the Turkish restaurant and had a satisfying meal. They really treated us well. Dinner done, we took a walk on the wild side and strolled the street, traveling farther away from our hotel. It was a fascinating, dangerous city, full of history going back thousands of years. Even though it was late, the shops were still open, and there was a fair amount of traffic in the streets. But after a while, I felt we had pushed our luck enough and insisted we get back to our hotel.

At one o'clock in the morning, I was awakened by the sound of more explosions. Alarmed, I jumped out of bed and went to the window. Of all things, there was a fireworks show going on—just like you'd see at a Fourth of July celebration—with skyrockets galore. It lasted for half an hour. A fireworks show in the middle of the night, in this war-torn, shot-up country. There was no one I could ask about it.

The following morning, our brothers picked us up as promised. I have no doubt they saved our lives. Once we got to the airport, the brothers walked us into the small terminal building, and we said our goodbyes amid many hugs. We had been touched by their hospitality, and they had been blessed by our visit. They informed us that we were the first Americans to step foot in their church since 1981.

Mike and I grabbed something to eat at an espresso shop in the airport and even bought a few souvenirs. Security was tight as we began moving towards our gate, not surprisingly. They made me open my suitcase, and I wondered what the guy must have thought about me having an almost empty bag. Oh well.... At least I could relax that they wouldn't arrest me for that. Probably.

There was an air-conditioned lounge area after the initial x-ray machines and metal detectors. But when it came time to move to the boarding area, we left the air conditioning behind us, and the heat level rose dramatically. We entered the long hallway and got into a line which led to the second security check at the boarding gate itself. There was no central air conditioning at all here. Every seventy-five feet, there were standing air conditioner units about the size and shape of an American gas station pump, but they did no good at all unless you stood right in front of them. The line was long. Directly in front of me was a tiny, young Muslim woman, probably in her late twenties. She couldn't have weighed more than a hundred pounds. She wore the traditional long sleeves and head covering. I didn't envy her in this heat. As the people at the front of the line got through the security check and moved into the boarding area, the line in front of us inched slowly forward. This small Muslim woman would push her suitcase forward, then leave the line and go over to stand in front of the closest air conditioning unit. I heard the people in line behind me chuckle each time she did this. She didn't care; she was suffering in this heat. She would position her face right up close to it and hold her arms up to it, getting as cool as she could in the short time before having to return to the line to move her suitcase forward. This pattern continued all the way down the hall. When the previous AC unit was too far away, she would begin using the next closest one farther forward. And so it went.

Finally, it was my turn to take everything out of my pockets, take my shoes off, and run all of it through the x-ray machine. It was a relief to be going out of the country instead of trying to get Precious Cargo into it. I could see Mike a long way behind me. He had stopped to buy something in one of the shops. After making it through security, putting my belt on, and making sure I had my cell phone and all my gear, I looked around for a place to sit. The young Muslim woman had three empty seats on one side of her, so I took the one in the middle. She sat on my left, and on my right, there were three solidly-built men with short haircuts. My mind immediately pegged them as military, and not Arabic. After a while, the man closest to me took out a cell phone and made a call. He said in a clear American voice, "Did everyone get through okay?" I kept a straight face, but I was shocked. These three men were American military. Perhaps they were private contractors or an American special forces unit. I would never know.

"Good," I heard him say. "Now all you have to worry about is jet lag." He listened another minute, then said, "Okay, we'll see you soon." He turned and gave his companions the update, and I could hear in their voices that all three were American. I would have given a lot to be able to ask them what they were doing in a hell-hole like this country, but then they'd be free to ask me the same thing. I couldn't jeopardize the lives of the Christians there by letting it be known that they were receiving outside help. All I could do was enjoy the moment of being in a place where few Americans had been, and let my imagination run wild about why these guys were here.

A few minutes later it got even more intriguing. The boarding call came over the loudspeaker, and to my astonishment, the young Muslim woman on my left jumped up, looked past me to the three American men, and in a heavy Arabic accent announced, "That's us. Let's go." They jumped to their feet, grabbed their bags, and followed her like obedient puppies. I'm still astonished to this day when I think back on that experience. I would have given a lot to know who she was and hear her story.

A few minutes later, Mike and I boarded, and the rest is history. Recently, my wife and I were driving across California, and to pass the time, we each picked our three favorite restaurants in which we had ever eaten, anywhere in the world. Then we went on to the list of our three favorite hotels where we had ever stayed. Then our three favorite travel destinations. When we had run out of ideas, I told her that my favorite travel experience of all time was when the wheels of my plane left the tarmac in the lion's den to bring me back home.

16

Plus One

Central African Republic is, as you might expect, right in the middle of Africa. In 2014, 1,088 Christians were killed there in a flurry of attacks by Muslims. Almost a million survivors, both Muslims and Christians, fled the fighting and ended up in refugee camps across the country. In March, 2015, I was part of a small team sent to reach out to the believers. In one camp we visited, which held 50,000 people, there were only three pastors. Those pastors had lost everything, just like all the other people in the camp, but they followed their calling by continuing to minister regardless of their circumstances.

C.A.R. is slightly smaller than Texas. In all the country, there is no electricity anywhere except the capital city of Bangui, and even there it is only on from 5 a.m. until 5 p.m. There is only one European flight into and out of C.A.R. each week. The plane lands on Tuesday, unloads, then picks up the passengers who are leaving and departs until the following week. There are no automated tellers (ATMs) in the country at all; so you have to take it in with you when you go. Otherwise, you will be starving before you can fly out again the following week.

After I bought my plane tickets, twelve more Christians were killed. This was not going to be a walk in the park. For the first time ever, I felt fear about going on a mission trip. Many times I thought of calling Mary and telling her to take my name off the list for this team. It would have been inconsequential if I had withdrawn, because there were only two slots allotted for Americans, and there were more than two who wanted to go. My slot would have been filled immediately with the next person on the waiting list. As I wrestled with fear versus a clear calling from God to go into places like this, He put strongly into my mind the passage from Esther 4:14 (NIV). Mordecai told Esther, "For if you remain silent at this time, relief and deliverance for the Jews will arise from another place, but you and your father's family will perish. And who knows but that you have come to your royal position for such a time as this?" Esther knew that anyone who entered into the king's presence without being summoned would be promptly executed unless he just happened to be in a good mood that day. Despite the risk, she moved forward into the work for which she had been uniquely prepared. Now I had to do the same. God had prepared me just as Jonah's fish for "such a time as this." Proverbs 24:10 (NIV) also came to mind, "If you falter in times of trouble, how small is your strength!" So I pushed the fear into the back of my mind, placed my trust completely in God, and moved forward in preparation for the trip.

Before we left, the C.A.R. office of our missions company requested we bring discipleship materials in French with us on the trip. C.A.R. had formerly been a French colony, so the language is commonly spoken there. I found a good source and decided to print out five copies to put into my luggage. Then my wife announced that we were going to print out "five plus one."

I said, "Okay, we'll print out six, if that's what you think we should do."

She said, "No. Five plus one." She's a bookkeeper, and brilliant with numbers, but I still thought I should remind her that five plus one makes a total of six. She then told me that God had strongly put it on her heart that I was to give the first five copies to the field office but keep one in my backpack because God was going to lead me to someone who needed his or her own copy of it. So, we printed out five plus one. I stuck "the one" in my backpack. In the days before I left, we began praying for someone whom we nicknamed "Plus One." We prayed that God would guide me to him or her and would shine His light into the darkness where they lived.

I met up with my travel buddy, Phillip, in Charles de Gaulle Airport in Paris, each of us having flown from our hometowns in America. From there we flew into Bangui. Phil's seat was in a different part of the plane from mine. During the long flight from Paris, I thought I'd go say hello and see how he was doing. But as I got closer, I saw that he was in deep conversation with a young man in the next seat, so I held off. I found out later that this man was a military contractor (a civilian under contract with the military). He was on his way to C.A.R. to begin a one-year job guarding the American embassy in Bangui. The United States no longer has enough military strength to guard its own embassies, so they hire mercenaries. Later, when we landed, I saw the contractor join with about a dozen other men, all of whom looked like they had been cut from a cookie cutter. They were all about thirty years old, five-feet-ten-inches tall, and one-hundred-seventy pounds. An older man dressed in camouflage met them, carrying a clipboard, and helped them through immigration.

Four things about arriving in C.A.R. were sobering beyond anything I had seen before in my travels. The first was that the local office of the missions company in C.A.R. sent an email to Mary, our American trip coordinator, asking for the names and phone numbers of our next of kin. This took my breath away. We had always given that information to our American office without giving much thought to it. Having the in-country hosts request it for themselves was sobering. The second was that the airline staff wouldn't let us off the plane at Bangui Airport unless we showed our boarding pass. The same plane was going to fly to Cameroon for its next stop, and they didn't want anyone getting off in C.A.R. by mistake. It was almost like they were asking us, "Are you really sure you want to be here? Think it through, because we aren't coming back to get you for a whole week." The third was that between the plane and the Customs office, there were two tents set up to screen all arrivals for Ebola. The fourth was that upon landing, I saw white soldiers everywhere, armed to the teeth. Some were part of the French Army, and others were United Nations units, both of them having a large presence there in C.A.R. to stop the fighting. In fact, if they hadn't shown up and taken control, the killing would still be going on. Everywhere I looked in the small airport, there were heavily armed soldiers carrying assault rifles in their hands, not slung casually over their shoulder.

As it turned out, there had been four of our team on the plane. Besides Phil and myself, there were two people from the United Kingdom, a man and a woman. I was surprised the missions company allowed a woman to go into such a dangerous area. But when I got to know her during our stay, I found out that she had been to other places equally dangerous. She was intrepid, with a great deal of experience in this kind of work.

We were met by two African men whom I will call David and Micah. They helped us fill out the Customs paperwork and helped load our luggage into their van. David was a resident of C.A.R. and a full-time worker for our host missions company. Micah was visiting from Cameroon and also worked for this same company. He had come to help in C.A.R. when the violence began. He had been a crucial spiritual leader there when the fighting was raging around them.

We could look across the parking lot of the airport and see a huge refugee camp right there, with people living beneath the wings of burnt-out aircraft. When the massacres began, people fled to the international airport, reasoning that someone would intervene there, if for no other reason than to save the airplanes and keep the runways open. It had been a vain hope. The fighting had been fierce here, and there were a great many burned out hulks of planes which didn't evacuate in time. Now the people used them as shelters, making them into dwellings they hoped would be temporary. Children played on the wings and swung from the aircraft skeletons.

We drove through the city over poorly maintained streets full of potholes. As with any developing country, the sides of the roads were packed with people selling whatever they could to make a living. And there were many shoppers. Micah reported that not long ago, the streets were totally deserted. People were afraid to come out of their homes for fear of being shot or hacked with machetes. It was good to see some life had returned to the city, but Micah speculated that if a car motor backfired, the streets would be empty again within seconds.

We arrived at a large compound which was surrounded by a high brick wall. A guard slid open the heavy gate to let us in. We drove about a quarter mile past many buildings, to the back of the compound. Here were a couple of two-story buildings which would be our home base for the next week. We had a nice dinner that evening and met two more of our crew who had flown in from other

African countries where the one-flight-per-week restriction didn't apply.

Our hosts gave us an orientation to bring us up to date on the current situation. There were four major armed groups still involved: the Muslim militants (known as Selekas), the United Nations, the French Army, and the anti-Balakas (the word "balaka" means "machete" in the local dialect; the Muslims who began this fighting used mostly machetes in their killing). The anti-Balakas were so-called Christians, but in reprisal for the Muslim Seleka attacks on their communities, they had thrown off any allegiance to the Prince of Peace. Now they were just killers, rapists, and thieves, victimizing everyone—not just Muslims, but often their own people. We met several pastors who had been robbed by them, and we interviewed two Christian women who had been raped by them. They were as much to be feared as any Muslim jihadist, despite having grown up in Christian homes. There was a fifth group, but they were largely ineffective due to their small numbers. These were the police, called the gendarmes. About all they could really do was to break up domestic squabbles or fights between neighbors. They tried to keep a low profile, being few in number compared to the main four groups.

Our first day in Bangui, we interviewed the head of the Evangelical Alliance, Rev. Nicolas Guerekoyame-Gbangou. The E.A. is an umbrella organization of forty-two different denominations which have bonded together for the common work of spreading the Gospel in Africa. It is headquartered in Kenya, but Rev. Nicolas is the leader in C.A.R. He told us what it had been like, being caught in the worst part of the fighting between the Selekas and the anti-Balakas. His compound had been hit by grenades six times as they hunkered down inside, praying for peace to come. Now that the U.N. and the French Army were there, the fighting had subsided. They were all praying that the peace would last.

Next, we toured the airport refugee camp. Parking on the outskirts, we were guided by Micah into the heart of it, where we met one of the pastors under a roof made of plywood and 4x4 wooden posts. This was what served as his church. It had no walls, just the roof to keep the hot African sun off him as he preached. On Sunday mornings, he led worship for two hundred fifty believers there. The pastor told us how he got his family out of their home as the mobs approached, burning every house in the Christian neighborhoods. Being a pastor for many years, he had owned a large library of books which he used in preparing his sermons. When his house was burned down, he lost all that and everything else they owned. Now he, his wife, and their two children lived here with all the other refugees in a shelter he had put together out of canvas.

We sat under the plywood roof, listening to his story as Micah translated. When he was finished, our teammate from Wales read him a passage from Isaiah 58:9-11 (NIV): "If you do away with the yoke of oppression…and if you spend yourselves in behalf of the hungry and satisfy the needs of the oppressed, then your light will rise in the darkness, and your night will become like the noonday. The LORD will guide you always; he will satisfy your needs in a sun-scorched land and will strengthen your frame." The African pastor began weeping, got up, walked across and knelt in front of the Welsh brother. Our group gathered around, laid hands on him, and prayed with him. He was exhausted from giving comfort to those who were hurting, having no one to give back to him in his own need.

When we finished praying, the pastor led us through the alleys and avenues between make-shift shelters, to his own tent. As we walked, hordes of children followed us, some holding onto our hands. Kids the world over adapt quickly, no matter the circumstances. Some of these were laughing and teasing each other, but most of them were obviously hungry. They were pulling on our hands and pleading one word which is the same in French and English, "sandwich," in the hope that we had brought them something to eat. It was heart-rending. We had nothing to give them. Even if we had had enough for a few, fighting would have broken out among them as the bigger kids took the food away from the smaller kids. This was beyond our ability to help.

Many of the families we passed came out to see us, and most of them were smiling. I didn't know if it was genuine goodwill toward us, or just a pleasant relief from the boredom in which they lived each monotonous day.

The pastor introduced us to his wife, who greeted us with a big smile. She held an infant in her arms and a second child peeked around her skirt with wide eyes. We only had a couple of minutes to interact with her before a delegation from the anti-Balakas showed up, ordering us that we had to pay hundreds of Euros if we wanted to interview these people. They controlled this camp, having morphed from a force dedicated to protecting Christians, to a kind of Mafia that was only looking to squeeze money from the situation, however they could. For many months, news crews from around the world had been showing up, bankrolled by foreign agencies and willing to pay whatever was necessary to get a good story. They assumed we were working for the same kinds of companies, flush with money to hand out. We weren't, so we had to leave or get hurt. Micah told us not to take any more pictures, and an anti-Balaka minion followed us out to our van to make sure of it.

On our second day in the country, we made a trip from the capital city of Bangui to a small town called Boda. It was less than two hundred miles, but the trip took a long time because the roads were so bad that sometimes we were reduced to three miles per hour. The hours went by slowly as we navigated the dirt road. It had rained a lot just before we got there, so there were large areas of mud. We passed several villages, and for a while we ran alongside a river. From time to time, we saw children playing in the water, and twice we saw women washing clothes.

Several times, we had to stop at military roadblocks. These were manned by African troops dressed in camouflage and carrying AK-47 rifles. The first time this happened, they ran us through a lot of bogus red tape and then asked to see our passports. I always carry my passport, as do most travelers, but the lady from England didn't have hers with her. She had reasoned, "We aren't crossing any foreign borders, so there isn't any need to bring it." She was right, but that gave the checkpoint guards the opening they were looking for. David, our local C.A.R. guide, had to negotiate a five Euro bribe with them. We later found out that this kind of thing is simply a fact of life in most African countries. An hour later, we came upon a makeshift roadblock set up by hopeful teenagers. They had no guns, so our driver merely waved at them imperiously, and they pulled the barricade out of the way.

We were in a Toyota Land Cruiser, and at one point we popped a tire. It wasn't a puncture. Rather the driver had been going too fast on this bad road, and when he hit a rock, the tire simply popped and lost all its air. He had been hired for the day and had never seen the vehicle prior to showing up for work that morning. We soon found out that although it had a spare tire, there was no lug wrench. So, the driver jogged back to the last village, while we stayed behind with the car and enjoyed the swarm of mosquitoes coming from the nearby swamp. It was an eerie feeling to be sitting helpless on a road where so many armed factions were hostile to outsiders. Our driver returned an hour later, riding on the back of a motorbike. The owner of the bike was bringing him to us for a fee. He was carrying lots of assorted wrenches which had been borrowed from other villagers. None of them fit the Toyota lug nuts. Finally, a Toyota pickup truck, full of gendarmes in the back, came along and stopped briefly to see what was going on. Since we were both in Toyotas, their lug wrench was a good fit, which was an answer to our prayer. They tossed it to us, but they were afraid to wait until we changed the tire, saying, "We can't stay. Just bring the wrench back to us in Boda." Since they are outgunned by all the different warring factions, they feared getting caught on this road, which was controlled by the anti-Balakas. As they drove away, I thought, "If the guys with the guns are scared, what does that say about us, with no guns?" I immediately remembered Psalm 108:12 (NIV), "Give us aid against the enemy, for human help is worthless." We got the tire changed and were on our way without further incident.

Later in the day, when we were just outside our destination of Boda, we came to the last roadblock. Our driver got out and went to talk with the guards. He was there quite a while. When he returned he chatted briefly with Micah, our trip leader. Micah burst out laughing, got out, and walked up to talk with the guards himself. After a few minutes, he came back, and we were on the road again. As a pleasant surprise, the guards were simply asking for Bibles of their own instead of money. Micah told them he'd bring some the next time he came this way.

We pulled into Boda just as the sun was setting. Arriving at a church which was our designated rendezvous point, we were met by a large contingent of pastors who had gathered to welcome Micah. He was a hero to them, having come from Cameroon to stand with them during the worst fighting. They sang a song in their language, which I couldn't understand, but I could see Micah was deeply touched.

We had a meaningful time of meeting with the Christians there, hearing their stories of all they had been through. It was two days of sweet—yet at times gut-wrenching—fellowship. Boda is a town of some twenty-five thousand people, about one-third of whom are Muslim. The main industry is diamond mining. Micah told us that the last time he was here, just a few months before, there had been sandbagged machine gun emplacements throughout the town. Their absence now marked a significant improvement in relations between the Christians and Muslims. It looked like any other normal town, at this point. However, we learned from the main government military leader headquartered in Boda, that there were still some six thousand people living out in the bush, too traumatized to return home.

At one point during our two days there, we toured the Christian section of town which had been burned in the fighting. As I tried to get a better view of one devastated church building, I pushed through some tall brush. Only when I got back in the van did I look down at my pant legs. If I had not been wearing thick canvas "firehose" pants and high-topped leather boots, I'd have been in serious pain. My pant legs looked like a porcupine had attacked them. There were hundreds of long thorns sticking in them. As Micah and I worked together to pull them out, I thought of those six thousand people living in the bush among thorn bushes like the ones I had walked through, drinking contaminated water, and starving, too scared to come home.

Our purpose for being in Boda was to minister to the Christians there. We listened to their stories of the hardships they had faced and of the loved ones they had lost. My travel buddy Phil asked the pastors he interviewed how many of them had lost family members during the fighting. Eighty percent of them raised their hands. They wanted outsiders to hear their stories, so we listened for hours. And when they were done, we offered encouragement from God's word, and we prayed with them. Nothing we could offer would take away their pain, nor relieve their suffering, but it mattered to them that we had come so far just because we cared. As has been said many times, showing up is half the battle.

During the fighting, the anti-Balakas had taken over the mosque in Boda. They wanted revenge for the churches which had been burned and for the Christians who had been killed. We heard the story from one of the pastors about how he had gone down and talked serious Christianity to the anti-Balakas who were occupying the place. He reminded them we are to love our enemies and do good to those who persecute us, that Jesus had sent us out as sheep among wolves. In the end, he won out and they vacated the mosque. The pastor called the imam on his cell phone and told him he could come back and retake ownership of his place of worship. The Muslims in Boda were so moved by this act of love that they made peace with the Christians here in this one small corner of C.A.R.

They invited us to their mosque to tell us the story and express their gratitude. We were happy to accept.

We had been told to bring cots if at all possible, so we wouldn't have to sleep on the ground. I had found one in a sporting goods store which came apart easily and fit into my suitcase. Thankfully, I didn't have to use it. Our group was offered the use of a large, air-conditioned house owned by a Muslim diamond merchant. It was powered by a gasoline generator. The man had fled to Bangui during the fighting and was now staying there, not at all sure the fighting was really over. In any case, it was wonderful that he extended his hospitality to Christians like us.

The second evening, as we met with the local pastors, a wasp the size of my index finger flew into the room. I didn't know they got that big anywhere in the world. I thought that if its sting was painful in proportion to how much bigger it was than its American counterpart, I'd give a lot to avoid being stung by it. I looked around the table where eight other men sat listening to the pastor tell of having been robbed of his motorbike by an anti-Balaka militant, and no one but me seemed to care about this flying dinosaur-wasp which hovered over us. No matter, I lost all track of the pastor's story, my attention now riveted on the possibility of dying from an African wasp sting. My life's priorities changed in an instant; now the priorities were, number one: serving Jesus; number two, avoid being stung by this wasp; and number three, everything else. It flew around, landed, then took off into the air again. Once I lost track of it for a moment, then it flew up from behind my shoulder and began going in circles again. After several minutes of this, one of the local pastors across the table suddenly grabbed a magazine from the table, stood up, and knocked the wasp out of the air onto the ground. He stepped on it before it could recover. Around the table, there was a collective sigh of relief. Much to my amusement, all the other guys had been just as worried about it as I had been. They were just better at faking it and pretending to be focused on what the speaker was saying. We went back to listening to him. But a moment later, another wasp flew in and began threatening us. This time there was no attempt at nonchalance. We declared war on it immediately, and it died quickly. Then another one flew in, and another. Finally, Micah took matters in hand and left the room, coming back in with an old-fashioned pump spray tube like I saw when I was a kid in Texas, the kind used to spray against mosquitoes. He sprayed the whole room, and we weren't bothered by wasps any more, just the fog of poisoned air in which we now sat.

On the return trip from Boda to Bangui, our cook, Mama Ruth, wanted to buy vegetables, so we stopped in a village which had a nice selection right there by the road. As she bargained with the villagers through the open doors in the back of the Land Cruiser, I heard a man outside my window say, "Hey mister, look." Since our vehicle had no air conditioning, we had been traveling with the windows open, so there was nothing between him and myself. I turned to see a man holding up his thumb, which was bleeding.

My first thought was, "Hey, I have a first aid kit in my backpack. I'll treat this guy's wound."

As I got the kit out of the pack, Micah, a greatly respected man of God, said to me, "Stop what you are doing." I stopped, surprised. Micah had shown himself to be a man worthy of being obeyed, so although I didn't understand this, I sat looking at him, waiting for the next development. His words carried a lot of weight, because, among other things, he had taught a Forgiveness and Reconciliation Seminar in Boda the previous year during the worst part of the fighting. Finally, he continued, "He is showing you that he has cut a white man." This put things in a whole new light, and I sat there stunned, wondering how to proceed.

Finally, I said, "That may be, but he still has a wound that may get infected, and I have the kit to treat it."

Micah replied, "Do not care about him. His friends standing behind him are saying, 'They are here to steal our diamonds.'" Now I realized how serious the situation was. We had heard many testimonies from pastors and their wives about friends who had been killed, and we had seen the burned-out ruins of their homes in Boda. Now it all became even more real. We were right in the middle of a war zone in which the fighting had subsided briefly, but was still smoldering beneath the surface, ready to burst into flame again at any moment.

I obediently zipped my pack closed and sat there facing away from the window as the man outside kept saying, "Hey mister, look. Hey you. Hey, look," for what seemed like an eternity, as I prayed for our protection. Finally, Mama Ruth was done, and she closed the doors enabling us to get moving.

We were all delighted to get out of that village, but our relief was short-lived. About fifteen minutes later, our motor ran out of oil and began making loud, expensive noises until it finally just shut down. We got out and pushed, trying to get it started, but to no avail. We were once again left behind (in swarms of flies this time) while the driver jogged to the next village ahead.

Going back to the previous village would have been suicidal. After a long time, he returned, once again on the back of a motorbike, carrying a large container of oil. He poured the oil into the motor, and cranked it over for a long time, no doubt further damaging it. Finally, we pushed it again and, much to my astonishment, it started—only now with much loud banging. The motor continued to clang and clack, metal on metal, as we made it a few miles more. It died permanently in the middle of another village. Our hearts sank, thinking back to the previous village and wondering how bad this was going to get. I thought, "This may be where my earthly life ends. Ah well, I always knew there was a chance of this happening on any one of these trips. In any case, there's no better way to die than while working for Jesus, trying to bring relief to hurting brothers and sisters. This isn't going to be fun, but God will be with us in whatever happens here."

Micah tried to call to Bangui for help, but there was no cell phone reception at all in that village. The locals all turned out to watch the new entertainment, and they helped push the Toyota uphill and back downhill in the vain hope that it might start again without major repair. I stood in the shade of a large tree next to the road and watched the futility.

So…we were stuck in the middle of one of the worst parts of Africa, on a road controlled by the anti-Balaka renegades, with no cell phone reception. How bad was this going to get?

Trying to get the Land Cruiser started was obviously not going to work. Eventually, I made the recommendation to Micah that we put David (our in-country guide from Bangui) on one of the motorbikes which were in the village and send him to a high point where he could perhaps get cell phone reception and call home to ask for someone to come rescue us. He held off for a while, hoping for a miracle, then finally acquiesced, putting David on the back of a motorbike (for a fee to the owner of the bike, naturally) and sending him uphill. We felt better, knowing help would be on the way.

The locals, surprisingly, were friendly and brought out comfortable wooden chairs for us to sit in the shade under a big tree.

This was a shock, considering the previous village. These people were friendly, although they held back from talking with us, probably due to shyness with strangers. Some time later, I spied David far up the hill, walking back without the motorbike. When he finally reached us, we found out the motorbike had suffered a flat tire. He had been unable to call for help. This was becoming comical now. Hours had passed and still no one knew of our situation, so there was still no help on the way. We hired another motorbike and David set off once more.

After sitting in those comfortable wooden chairs for about an hour, a young man approached me, and speaking French, he said "Bible?" I felt bad, not having one I could offer him. Then it dawned on me. This was Plus One! I didn't have a Bible to give him, but I did have a thirty-page discipleship manual (in French) which covered everything necessary, from who Jesus is, through the basics of salvation, all the way through what it meant to serve God with one's whole heart throughout life, up to becoming a pastor and running a church.

I answered, "Wait just a second," while I dug it out of my pack and gave it to him. As I watched him walk away reading it, my tears began to flow. I was seeing the fulfillment of God's plan unfold right in front of me.

I turned to the other men sitting there under the shade tree with me and told them, "God didn't just allow this breakdown; He orchestrated it perfectly. This is why we broke down, right here in this exact place. God was guiding us to this village, to this young man. God left nothing at all to chance. This began weeks ago, all the way back in America, with my wife insisting I keep an extra copy of this material in my backpack without turning it over to the Bangui office. It was just for this village. God is doing something in this country and in this area, and we have just seen it begin."

We turned around to see where the young man had gone with the packet I had given him. He was sitting behind us with three of his friends, all of them huddled over the manual, going over it intensely. Later, when I turned to look again, he was gone and so was the manual. He had taken it into his house. I have no doubt he had been praying for divine guidance, and now God had sent me with exactly what this Christian village had been needing.

As we sat there all afternoon, an older man came up and introduced himself to us in French. He was the pastor of the

Christian church of this village. It was within a hundred yards of where we sat. In fact, God had stopped our Toyota exactly in front of the pastor's house. He wanted to show us his church, so we were blessed to walk over and see where the Gospel was preached every Sunday in that village. Plus One accompanied us, still clutching the discipleship packet in his hand.

David returned soon to tell us he had gotten through, and help was on the way. Now, all we had to do was wait.

During the afternoon, a man came by trying to sell the skin of a crocodile. Numerous little boys played with wooden trucks someone had carved for them. Many women and girls came by carrying heavy loads on their head in classic African style. The women of the households were beating cassava roots into a paste for their evening dinner, and some of them chopped firewood. Meanwhile, we nursed our water bottles, because the ones in our hands were the only ones left of the sixty we had started our journey with two days earlier. They had to last us the rest of the way home.

As the sun began to set, and our villagers began to filter back to their homes for dinner, a man I will call Barnabas, of the Bangui office, arrived in a Toyota crew-cab pickup to rescue us. We transferred all our gear to the bed of the pickup. Six of us crammed into the crew cab, and Mama Ruth climbed into the pickup bed on top of our gear along with our former driver. I protested vigorously that Mama Ruth should ride up front and I could ride in the bed of the truck but was told firmly by Micah that I would not win this argument, given the nature of African hospitality to visitors. I finally gave up and climbed into the cab.

After the three-hour drive, it was 9:20 p.m. when we pulled into our compound in Bangui. It had been an incredible day.

Getting out of the country at the end of our week proved to be an adventure in itself. We had to go through checkpoints manned by United Nations troops who were heavily armed. They checked the passports of everyone in the van before letting us through into the airport parking lot. Once inside the airport, French army soldiers were everywhere. Evidently, the two armies divided the labor: the United Nations troops handled access to the airport, while the French army handled security within.

We had to pay a fee of 10,000 francs for a stamp on our boarding pass. That was about twenty American dollars. They were clearly charging us to leave their country. All I could think of was that it's worth whatever it takes to get out of here. There was no air conditioning in the terminal and the heat was fierce. Then came the security checks. We had to go through several, and the security people took whatever they wanted from our carry-on bags. One female guard "confiscated" a hair dryer from our only female team member. Another guard took the beef jerky Phillip was carrying to share on our long layover in Cameroon. And so it went. I was fortunate; they didn't want anything I had.

After a long wait in the stifling hot waiting area, a bus pulled up. As we went out to get on, there was yet another security check. They went through all the bags again, including my fanny pack, and all our pockets. It was a lengthy procedure, but finally we were done and were driven out to the waiting jet. As we stowed our carry-ons in the overhead bins, I noticed a lady in a seat nearby who had made conversation with me on our incoming flight the previous week. We exchanged greetings, and then she asked if I had heard the shootout last night. I hadn't. French soldiers had had a running gunfight with persons unknown right outside the apartment where she was staying. It didn't last too long, and the shots faded into the distance as the chase got farther away. Evidently, that's just life in Bangui.

We got all buckled in, then sat there. And sat there. The pilot came on the speaker, eventually, and said we were having mechanical difficulties. It had already been late in the afternoon when we boarded, and now it began to get dark. At five o'clock all the electricity in Bangui went off as usual, which made the airport go dark, except for a few lights which must have been powered by an emergency generator. This meant we had no runway lights by which to take off. I overheard two guys talking in the seats behind me. One was telling the other one that if we couldn't take off, we'd be stuck here until the U.N. could mobilize an armored convoy to come get us and take us to a safe place for the night.

Finally, the pilot announced the repairs had been made, but now he was having to contact Paris to get permission to take off in the dark. Did I mention I love adventure travel? Not long after that, the pilot got the clearance he needed and we took off. Evidently, this wasn't our pilot's "first rodeo," as they say in Texas. He was experienced in this kind of work, and we got into the air with no further problems.

We had a short flight to the next country to the west of C.A.R., Cameroon, where we landed and deplaned so the crew who had flown from Paris could end their shift, and the next crew could come aboard for the flight back to Paris. The airport staff had sandwiches and soft drinks for us, so we didn't mind the wait.

As groups gathered to pass the time, one lady struck up a conversation with me. She had been doing missionary work in C.A.R. for many years and knew the ropes. She told me the pilot having to ask Paris for permission to take off in the dark was a mere formality. It was common knowledge that any airplane left on the ground all night would be a heap of molten rubble by morning. One militia or another would burn it just for fun. There was never any doubt about Paris giving permission to take off.

The violence hasn't stopped since I left. On our first day in the country, we had interviewed the head of the Evangelical Alliance, Rev. Nicolas Guerekoyame-Gbangou. His office is located in a compound of high walls and the usual eight-foot-high sliding gate which only opens from the inside. Six months after we left, in September of 2015, he was targeted for assassination. A mob of attackers broke into the compound, but he had left thirty minutes earlier. The mob set his office on fire, then killed two displaced persons who had come there for protection from the violence.

Then, as I was writing this chapter in May of 2017, his brother and a nephew were killed in another attack by Muslims. Ten churches were either burned or looted, and more than one hundred eighty people were killed in various places around C.A.R. during this spasm of violence.

Even so Lord Jesus, come quickly.

17

When All Is Said and Done

I began making these trips to give to the persecuted Christians, but I found that I never came back home feeling I had given more than I had received. In fact, the proportions were lopsided in the opposite direction. Each of these trips were gifts from God directly to me. I wouldn't trade any one of them for another ten years of life here on earth.

The believers I met were always the salt of the earth. They frequently subsisted on next to nothing and experienced great tragedy on a regular basis. Despite this, they had the joy of the Lord in their hearts and were always willing to do whatever they could for us, often to their own detriment. Their hospitality was humbling, their fellowship fed my soul, and they had much to teach me.

After a few of these trips, I found an odd frame of mind had settled into me. I found I felt more at home with them, in their environments, than I did when I got back to my own church, in my own country. I have given much thought to why this should be, and I have finally realized it's because they "get it." They see truth, total commitment, and sacrificial living in a way few in my own country do. They have insight which is only gained by living in an environment where they expect a knock on the door by the police any minute, or a howling mob coming to burn them out of their homes, or denial of admission to university because they checked the box marked "Christian" on the application. So now I live in an odd conundrum: when I am interacting and worshipping with my brothers in Vietnam, or Bangladesh, or Ethiopia, or…or…. I am much more comfortable than I am now in American churches where I first discovered the reality of Jesus and can worship openly, for now.

God always stretched me on each trip, a little further than on the last one. I never came back home the same person I had been when I left. And that's quite a positive benefit.

I began this book by talking about how I wasn't like the other kids. Although that is true, I do not in any way mean to imply that only thrill-seeking adrenaline junkies can be used by God in foreign missions, or in any other kind of work for Him. He has made us each unique, for specific jobs, and the Bible tells us we all have our God-given gifts. He certainly "prepared a fish" in my case, but in truth, God is always preparing a fish, every minute, in every believer, all over the world. Each of His children is uniquely created to be His masterpiece (Ephesians 2:10, NLT). We are all designed to be particularly suited for the places we are assigned to go, for the work we are given to do. As we follow our gifts, we will be guided into work we will love, because that's how He puts our personalities together. It's just how God works.

I wasn't led into this kind of work because I was braver or stronger than anyone else. In fact, my left leg is partly disabled, with limited strength. I can walk slowly over long distances because of having semi-successful surgery, but I can't run at all. And the leg is constantly cramping. On top of that, I was diagnosed with diabetes and sleep apnea before I ever went on my first mission trip. I need a CPAP machine to help me breathe when I sleep. I wear hearing aids, or I won't understand what folks are saying, even when they are right next to me. I could be the poster child for the passages in 2 Corinthians 12:9 and 1 Corinthians 1:27 (NIV): "His power is made perfect in my weakness," and "God chose the weak things of the world to shame the strong…." In the days when I thought I was indestructible, I accomplished nothing of value, ever. Once God broke me (Psalm 119:67), He was able to use me. As I've heard it said by many others, God doesn't care about our ability, just our availability.

I love Jesus's words in Luke 17:7-10 (NIV): "Suppose one of you has a servant plowing or looking after the sheep. Will he say to the servant when he comes in from the field, 'Come along now and sit down to eat'? Won't he rather say, 'Prepare my supper, get yourself ready and wait on me while I eat and drink; after that you may eat and drink'? Will he thank the servant because he did what he was told to do? So you also, when you have done everything you were told to do, should say, 'We are unworthy servants; we have only done our duty.'" And that is the bottom line in my case. I have only done my duty.

This has been the story of my own journey, but we are all on journeys and each of us has a story to tell.

For pictures and more information visit:
https://www.godpreparedafish.com

173

77915598R00104

Made in the USA
San Bernardino, CA
30 May 2018